Floral Designs for Cakes

Floral Designs for Cakes

Cynthia Venn

MEREHURST

LONDON

I should like to thank my husband, Rob, for all the help he has willingly given. Thanks also to Graham Tann for his inspired photography and for his friendly co-operation in achieving the results I wanted, and to the rest of the production team for their valuable contributions.

Note
Quantities of royal icing, sugarpaste, buttercream and almond paste are given in metric, imperial and US cup measurements. The weight of royal icing and sugarpaste refers to the quantity of icing (confectioner's) sugar required. The weight of buttercream and almond paste refers to the total weight of the butter and dry ingredients.

Published 1989 by Merehurst Limited
Ferry House, 51-57 Lacy Road
Putney, London, SW15 1PR

© Copyright 1989 Merehurst Limited

Reprinted 1990, 1991

ISBN 1 85391 051 1

Edited by Alison Leach
Designed by Clive Dorman
Photographed by Graham Tann, assisted by Lucy Baker
Typeset by Vision Typesetting, Manchester
Colour separation by J. Film, Bangkok
Printed in Singapore by C. S. Graphics

The cakestands displayed in the book are available from:

Cynthia Venn
3 Anker Lane
Stubbington
Fareham
Hants PO14 3HF

CONTENTS

FOREWORD

Cake icing and decorating are daunting tasks to the beginner – especially as they often involve intricate handiwork and craftsmanship. But as the old saying goes 'practice makes perfect', and once you've mastered the art, there's no end to creativity! If on the way you have the luck to learn the tricks of the trade from an expert in her own field like Cynthia Venn, winner of countless major icing awards, things become a lot easier.

Her book offers sound advice, easy to follow step-by-step photographs and beautiful finished results. Whether you're a novice or cake maker extraordinaire, you will find the ideas are original and inspiring.

Floral designs, whether simple or elaborate, always look impressive and are so versatile. You can use them for decorating all sorts of special occasion cakes – wedding, birthday, christening, anniversary or novelty – the skill lies in making the flowers look like the real thing! It therefore gives me great pleasure to recommend Cynthia Venn's latest book. It not only taught me a lot of new techniques but also sparked off endless ideas – I know it will have the same effect on you!!

SARAH GATES
Cookery Editor
Essentials

INTRODUCTION

Flowers are loved by everyone all over the world. They convey messages which do not require words, expressing feelings of love, sympathy, remorse and joy. They are precious for their beauty, perfume, powers of healing and certain culinary uses. In their natural state, they herald the new seasons.

The pagans warded off evil spirits with flowers. We use them now to brighten otherwise drab surroundings, to decorate our homes, churches, public buildings and ourselves. No celebration is complete without flowers. Their beauty has inspired many of the world's great painters, and poems and songs have also been written in tribute to them.

The trend for using sugar flowers, rather than fresh or fabric ones, to decorate cakes has grown in popularity in the British Isles during the past ten years. We have learned much from our friends in Australia and South Africa, at the same time adding our own ideas, new techniques and our native flowers so that, hopefully, we may give something to them in return.

I have included many of the old favourites in this book and have also introduced some new ideas of my own using, for instance, wild flowers. The floral theme has been interpreted not only with moulded flowers but also through various embroidery methods. In some cakes, the two techniques have merged in one design.

I hope that I have, in a small way, stimulated your imagination, encouraging you to experiment with other ways of using flowers in cake decoration.

CYNTHIA VENN

SPECIAL TECHNIQUES

FLOWER MODELLING PASTE

Use this mixture when the weather is humid or if you wish the flowers to remain in good condition for a long time.

450g (1lb/3 cups) icing
  (confectioner's) sugar
10ml (2 tsp) cornflour (cornstarch)
15ml (1 tbsp) gum tragacanth
10ml (2 tsp) powdered gelatine
25ml (5 tsp) cold water
10ml (2 tsp) white vegetable fat
10ml (2 tsp) liquid glucose
1 egg white, size 2 (large)

Sift the sugar, cornflour (cornstarch) and gum tragacanth into an ovenproof bowl. Heat gently in the oven or over a pan of boiling water until the sugar feels warm.

Sprinkle the gelatine on to the water and leave to stand until the gelatine has absorbed all the water. Then dissolve over hot water or in a microwave. Do not allow the mixture to boil as this would destroy the elasticity. Remove from the heat and add the fat and liquid glucose.

Pour the liquids and the egg white into a well in the centre of the sugar mixture. Mix in a heavy-duty electric mixer on the slowest speed until the sugar has been incorporated. Increase the speed to maximum and mix until the paste is white and stringy. This will take about 5–10 minutes.

Put the paste into a strong polythene bag and keep this in a lidded container in the refrigerator overnight. As this paste dries out quickly, it must be kept covered. To use, cut off only the small quantity required and store the remaining paste in the refrigerator.

FLOWER MODELLING PASTE (EASY)

white vegetable fat
5ml (1 tsp) gum tragacanth
225g (8oz/1 cup) commercial
  sugarpaste

Grease your hands with a little white fat and then knead the gum tragacanth into the sugarpaste. Store in an air-tight container and leave to rest overnight before using. It is not necessary to refrigerate this paste.

BRUSH EMBROIDERY

This is a very versatile technique enabling the decorator to produce attractive designs quite simply and quickly. By allowing a little more time to highlight and shade the finished design, really beautiful, delicate results are possible, giving much artistic satisfaction.

A white design on a white background is most suitable for a wedding cake, making a very elegant decoration. This is a good way of carrying the theme of any moulded flowers through to the rest of the cake, giving a well-balanced result.

A dramatic effect may be achieved by piping a white design on a dark background, but the most beautiful designs are those in which several complementary colours are used and delicately highlighted with diluted food colouring when the icing has completely dried.

Transfer the design to the cake or plaque by making a template and scribing the outlines. Outline individual sections of the design with a No1 nozzle, pipe an inner line and then brush the section with a damp paintbrush from the outer edge through to the base.

Work on the background first, completing one small section at a time and gradually working to the foreground. The edges should be the thickest part, fading to just a wash at the base. Use long, even strokes to avoid ridges and always brush leaves and petals in the direction which would be taken by the natural veining.

TUBE EMBROIDERY

Any of the traditional embroidery stitches may be used in tube embroidery and most of the instructions you will need can be found in needlecraft books.

Only four stitches have been used in the embroidery designs in this book:

> Long and short stitch for large leaves and petals
> Satin stitch for furled edges and for small petals
> Chain stitch for some small leaves
> Stem stitch for stems

Before starting to embroider a design, mix up all the colours and shades of icing that you will need. Put small

1 Design transferred to plaque petals, brushed from top to base
2 Background leaves and back
3 Front petals brushed through
4 Foreground petals completed, then furled edge, finally stamens

amounts of the different colours in greaseproof paper piping bags with No0 nozzles. Use small bags and do not more than half-fill them; this will allow more freedom of movement and greater accuracy as you will be working closer to the design.

Start with the background and begin to work towards the front. Complete one section at a time, changing the shade where necessary before starting another part of the design.

If the stitches are uneven, draw a damp brush through them to smooth out any rough areas.

FLOODED COLLARS

The icing used for collar work must not contain any glycerine. It should not be too old as the icing relaxes too much and looks rather wet; the run-out pieces are also very slow to dry. The appearance will not be as glossy as that achieved with fresh icing.

Icing made in an electric mixer should be allowed to stand at least 24 hours and then stirred vigorously with a wooden spoon to disperse the air bubbles before using.

Some food colourings, particularly paste ones, contain some glycerine. These should be used with caution as the glycerine will make the icing remain soft.

Place the waxed paper or plastic wrap over the pattern, smooth it out and secure with icing or masking tape, ensuring that there are no creases.

Outline the collar with a No1 nozzle, then flood the centre with softer icing.

To make run-out pieces stronger, add a little more albumen dissolved in water or egg white to icing of normal piping consistency. The icing should be soft enough to produce a smooth, fine run-out. If it is too runny, it will flow over the side of the outline. If it is too thick, it will produce an uneven surface.

Half-fill a vegetable parchment piping bag with the soft icing and snip a small hole in the end. Do not use a nozzle for flood-work.

Fill the outline generously with the softened icing to make substantial run-out pieces with slightly domed surfaces. Use a paintbrush to coax the icing into any awkward little corners. Break any bubbles with the brush as soon as they appear on the surface.

To obtain a good sheen on collars and plaques, dry as quickly as possible near a gentle heat such as a radiator or under a lamp. Store on waxed paper until required.

When flooding a large collar to go all round a cake, first flood a small area, then go back to the beginning and add some icing to the other side. Continue in this way until the collar is complete. This will avoid there being an unsightly mark where the soft icing meets that which has already dried.

MAKING FLOWERS AND LEAVES

AZALEA

1 Tape seven fine stamens and one longer one to a 26g wire.

2 Cut out three petals in flower modelling paste with an azalea cutter. Frill the top edges with a cocktail stick (toothpick) or modelling tool. Press each petal on a veiner to mark it; a maize husk or cocoa pod may be used. Brush a little egg white on the right-hand side of the lower petal. Place the second and third petals in a line, slightly overlapping each other, sticking with egg white.

3 Cut out two more petals. Frill, vein and stick together as before.

4 Brush pale pink petal dust on to the petals, leaving the frilled edges white.

5 Wrap the group of three petals around the stamens using egg white as an adhesive and leave to set. To keep the shape, invert a large-holed icing nozzle, push the stamens through the hole and leave the nozzle to support the upside-down petals.

6 Dab a little egg white on the base of the two petals and attach in the gap in the group of three. Leave to dry in a

flower support or a foil cone, supporting the petals with small pieces of foam if necessary.

7 One petal should be lying on top of the others. This petal and half of the petals on either side may be dotted with darkish red if desired but the remaining petals should be left plain.

BELLFLOWER

Otherwise called campanula, there are many types of bellflower including cultivated varieties, but one of the loveliest is the harebell, also known as the bluebell of Scotland. They can be found in blue, purple and white. The harebell dances on the end of a long slender stem and, unlike some of the other bellflowers, hangs its head. The basic instructions are the same for all members of this plant family.

1 Mould a ball of flower modelling paste into a Mexican hat shape and roll out the flat edge thinly with a knitting needle.

2 Cut out the flower with a medium blossom cutter and push a pointed modelling tool into the centre to form a throat. Press the base with a finger to keep the bell-shape and open up with a small ball tool. Flute each petal with a cocktail stick (toothpick) or Dresden tool. Pinch the petals to point them.

3 Make a hook in a fine covered wire. Push a tiny ball of paste deep into the throat of the flower to cushion the wire and insert the moistened wire through the paste and out of the base of the throat.

4 Add fine stamens and dust the centre with a touch of yellow.

5 To make the buds, take a small piece of paste, about half the size of the flower, and roll between the fingers to a

point. Insert a hooked wire. Thin the base of the bud by rolling between your fingers and paint the calyx.

6 To make the calyx for the flowers, use the smallest star calyx cutter to cut out the shape. Draw out the points with a dogbone modelling tool and pinch to make them long and thin. Dab egg white in the centre and slip over a hooked wire. Attach a tiny ball of green-coloured paste to the base of the calyx for the seed pod.

1 Roll a small ball of yellow-coloured flower modelling paste into a teardrop shape. Insert a hooked 26g wire into the pointed end of the centre.

2 To make the stamens, wrap yellow cotton around two fingers several times to make loops. Insert a piece of fine rose wire and twist firmly. Trim the cottons to the correct length. Repeat twice. Arrange the three sets of stamens evenly around the rose centre and tape them all together.

3 Cut five petals with a medium rose petal cutter. Cut a V in each round edge to make heart-shaped petals. Flute the edges and cup the centre with a ball tool. Arrange the petals over a small domed shape, such as the back of a teaspoon, until partially dry.

4 Place a tiny ball of paste in the base of a greased apple tray (as used in supermarkets). Slightly overlap the petals and stick with egg white. The petals will form a spiral and the last petal should be tucked under the edge of the first one. Moisten the centres of the petals with egg white and push the wired stamens into the centre. Leave the rose in the apple tray until completely dry. Then remove and attach the calyx.

CARNATION

Carnations and other frilly flowers look more delicate when the edges of the petals are dusted with a deeper or contrasting colour.

1 Fold a stamen in half, cut off the tips and tape or wire them to the end of a piece of 26g covered wire.

2 Roll out some flower modelling paste very thinly. Cut out a petal with a carnation cutter. Make small cuts around the edge.

3 Dust a board with cornflour (corn-

starch). Lay the petal on the board and frill by rolling the tip of a cocktail stick (toothpick) backwards and forwards over the edge.

4   Brush the centre of the petal with egg white. Insert a wire into the centre. Fold the petal in half with the stamen cottons protruding. Brush one side of this folded petal with egg white and fold into the middle with the frilled edge in line. Turn the petal over and brush the other side with egg white. Repeat, folding to the opposite side.

5   Cut two more petals. Prepare as before. Brush egg white in the centre, push the wire through and allow the second petal to fall over the first one. Press the base to secure. Repeat with the third petal. Leave to dry. If the petals have a tendency to fall away from the centre, dry the flower by hanging it upside-down.

6   To make the calyx, mould a pea-sized ball of green-coloured paste into a Mexican hat shape. Cut out with a star calyx cutter. Hollow the calyx by pressing a pointed modelling tool into it. Thin the points. Moisten with egg white and push the wire of the flower through the centre.

CHRISTMAS ROSE

1   To make the centre, roll a small piece of pale green-coloured flower modelling paste into a teardrop shape. Flatten the top and insert a 26g hooked wire into the base. Stick numerous short stamens around the centre, brush the tips with egg white and dip into yellow-coloured cornmeal or sugartex.

2   Roll out some white paste very thinly and cut out five petals with a medium rose petal cutter. Thin the edges with a dogbone modelling tool, elongating the petals by drawing the tool from the base to the tip. Vein by pressing against a piece of maize husk, a cocoa pod or similar object.

3   Place a small disc of paste in a former or chocolate mould. Add the petals, sticking each one with egg white and overlapping them. Tuck the edge of the last petal under the first one.

4   Brush egg white into the centre and insert the stamens on the wire. Lightly dust the centre of the flower with green blossom tint. When dry, remove from the former and brush the back of the flower with pale green blossom tint.

5   Cut two bracts from thinly rolled green-coloured paste, using a miniature rose petal cutter. Thin the edges and cup. Alternatively, these bracts could be cut from flower tape. Tape one bract just under the flower, twist the stem tape a few turns around the stem and attach the second bract on the opposite side and about 6-mm ($\frac{1}{4}$-in) lower than the first.

CYMBIDIUM ORCHID

There are many varieties of cymbidium orchids and just as many colours, so it is advisable to consult a reference book to take advantage of the lovely shades.

1 Curve a piece of 24g hooked wire over the fleshy part of your thumb.

2 Shape a ball of flower modelling paste into a teardrop and mould around the wire, which has been moistened with egg white. This forms the column.

3 Hollow the underside of the column with a dogbone modelling tool and pinch two little scallops at the front edges, keeping the curved shape.

4 Stick a small ball of white paste to the front of the column with egg white. Press a knife into the centre of the ball to divide it into two lips. Paint spots on the underside and leave to dry.

5 Roll out some paste very thinly and cut out the trumpet. Flute the front edge with a cocktail stick (toothpick). Work the side edges with a ball tool until thin and curved inwards. Shape over an orchid former or in a bed of cotton wool and leave until firm but not completely dry.

6 Roll a tiny piece of yellow-coloured paste into a cigar shape. Attach to the back of the throat with egg white. Press a cocktail stick into the centre to flatten and divide into two.

7 Moisten the back point of the trumpet and attach the column to it. This should fit neatly but do not close the trumpet over the column.

8 Cut out three lateral sepals with the larger of the petal cutters. Roll out some paste very thinly, leaving a thicker base in which to insert the wire. Vein the sepals with an orchid veiner or maize husk. Soften the edges with a dogbone modelling tool and insert a 33g wire which has been dipped in egg white. Leave to dry completely over a curved shape. The back sepal should curve towards the centre of the flower.

9 Cut out the two side petals and repeat the procedure. Dry over a curved shape. Paint or dust shading on the petals and sepals. Paint the trumpet.

10 Bend the wires at right angles to the sepals. Assemble the flower by taping together the lateral sepals; the back one should curve forwards.

11 Add the side petals which should lie in front. Tape securely.

12 Add the trumpet and tape the stem securely.

DAISY

The daisy, which is one of the prettiest English wild flowers, is quite simple to make but special care should be taken when making the calyx which consists of many pointed bracts cupping the flower head. If possible, examine a real daisy.

1 Make a hollow in a tiny ball of green-coloured flower modelling paste by inserting a cocktail stick (toothpick) and rolling from side to side. Cut many V-shaped notches around the edge. Insert a fine hooked wire dipped in egg white and re-shape the base.

2 Roll out some white paste very thinly and cut out the petals with a daisy petal cutter. Divide each petal by cutting down the middle. Thin each petal by pressing down the centre with a cocktail stick.

3 Moisten the calyx with egg white and lay the petals centrally on it. Press

the centre with a ball tool to make a sightly concave shape.

4 Make a centre by rolling a small piece of deep yellow-coloured paste into a ball. Press this firmly into a piece of coarse net or wire mesh to represent the texture of the inner disc which is made up of many tiny florets. Moisten the centre of the petals and press in the yellow-coloured disc.

5 When dry, dust a little green blossom tint into the centre. The edges of the petals may be lightly dusted with pink if desired.

FRANGIPANI

1 Roll out some white flower modelling paste and cut out five petals with a frangipani or azalea cutter. Cover the petals with plastic wrap to prevent their drying out too soon.

2 Place the first petal in the palm of your hand and with a dogbone modelling tool gently stroke the left-hand side of the petal from the top to where it narrows – this edge should curve inwards. Repeat with the other four petals and leave until set but not too dry.

3 When the petals are holding their shape, brush a little egg white on the right-hand side of each petal at the base. Place the petals in an overlapping line, keeping the tops level as shown. Brush yellow petal dust on the base of each flower.

4 Holding the group of petals upside-down by the base in one hand, twist them away from you with the other hand, encouraging them to hold together. Stick the last petal in line to the back of the first petal.

5 Put the flower into a special flower stand. Alternatively, make a cone of foil, cut a hole in the bottom and place the cone in the neck of a bottle for support.

Open up the petals a little for a half-open flower or more for a fully open one.

6 When the flower is nearly dry, dip a hooked wire into egg white and press into the base. (If the arrangement is not to be wired, omit this step.)

7 When completely dry, dust the outside of the flower a pale pinky-brown.

HONEYSUCKLE

It is helpful to look at a cluster of real honeysuckle for greater accuracy.

1 Roll a pea-sized piece of flower modelling paste to form a narrow tube about 2.5-cm (1-in) long. Hollow and thin by inserting a cocktail stick (toothpick) and rolling across the board.

2 Make two long cuts to form a long thin petal. Pull forward away from the rest of the flower.

3 Cut a triangular section from each side of the flower to narrow it and cut three small notches to form four petals. Cut each petal to a point. Press between your thumb and finger to thin.

4 Insert a fine hooked wire through the centre. Roll the back between your fingers until it is long and very slender. Add five very fine stamens, one longer than the others. Curve the stamens over your finger.

5 Mould long buds as shown, keeping them small.

6 Brush the base of the flowers and buds with peachy-pink dust and a touch of yellow at the throat of each flower.

7 Tape the buds and flowers together

as shown. Attach tiny balls of green-coloured paste at the base of each flower.

LESSER CELANDINE

One of the first flowers to appear in spring, the lesser celandine is a strong yellow colour with a green tinge on the back of the petals.

1 To make the calyx, mould some green-coloured flower modelling paste into a small Mexican hat shape. Roll out very thinly at the edges using a knitting needle and cut out the calyx with a snowdrop cutter as this calyx has only three sepals. Cup with a ball tool.

2 Roll out some deep yellow-coloured paste thinly and cut out the flower with a daisy cutter. Thin and cup the petals with a dogbone modelling tool. Stick

centrally on the calyx with egg white.

3 Make cotton stamens (*see page 10*) and cut off fairly short. Tape together and insert through the centre of the flower. Spread the stamens out towards the petals.

4 Make a tiny green-coloured cone for the centre. Moisten the centre of the stamens and insert the cone, pressing firmly in position. Texture with the tip of a cocktail stick (toothpick).

5 When dry, dust the back of the flower with green/brown blossom tint and glaze the inside of the petals with gum arabic glaze.

LILY-OF-THE-VALLEY

A common garden flower which also grows wild in the British Isles. The numerous, sweet-smelling, bell-shaped flowers all hang on one side of the stem. A fine bract grows from the base of the flowers.

1 Roll some flower modelling paste into a tiny ball and mould into a Mexican hat shape.

2 Cut out the shape with a lily-of-the-valley cutter. Push a small ball tool deep into the flower, pressing the base with a finger to flatten and produce the bell shape. Press the edge of the petals against the ball tool to thin.

3 Moisten with egg white and insert the stamen. The stamen cottons look better when they are green; this can be achieved by dipping your finger and thumb into green petal dust and rolling the cotton between them until it becomes green.

4 Cut slivers from a piece of green flower tape for the bracts which grow just below the flowers.

5 Curve the stamen cottons by stroking with your finger nail.

6 Bind together numerous flowers on a wire in a hanging position, attaching a bract to the base of each flower.

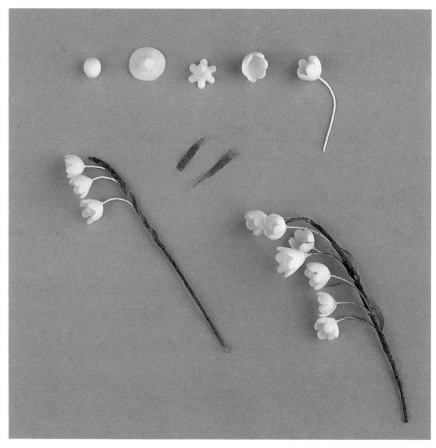

MORNING GLORY

Morning glory, bindweed and convolvulus all belong to the same plant family and only vary in colour and size. The method of making them in flower modelling paste is the same except for the leaves.

1 Roll a small marble-sized piece of blue-coloured flower modelling paste into a cylindrical shape.

2 Hollow by pressing an anger tool into the centre. Insert a cocktail stick (toothpick) deep into the hollow and

thin the paste by rolling the cocktail stick back and forth across the board. Continue rolling until you have a wide, funnel-shaped flower with thin fluted edges.

3 Insert a hooked 28g wire and neaten the back. With a veining tool, mark five ridges evenly all round from the base to the tip of the flower. Turn back the frilled edges and insert the stamens.

4 The calyx is in the form of a sheath which is in two parts. It may be made by

cutting out two shapes in light green-coloured paste with a miniature rose petal cutter. Thin the edges and tool into concave shapes. Attach both to the base of the flower, opposite each other.

5   The white centre and lines radiating from it are painted by mixing white petal dust with a little edible spirit and using this as paint. Finally dust a little yellow petal dust over the stamen area.

6   The buds are long and conical. The calyx is made as for the flower. Make a cone of paste about three-quarters the length of the flower and about 6-mm ($\frac{1}{4}$-in) in diameter. Insert a 28g wire and add the calyx. Mark the side of the cone with a sharp knife to represent the edges of the petals unfurling.

ORANGE BLOSSOM

This is a creamy white waxy flower with very prominent brown-tipped white stamens surrounding a pale green pistil. The stamens are joined in a continuous sheath at the base, dividing at the tip.

1   Make a pistil with pale green-coloured flower modelling paste. Insert a 28g hooked wire and dust the tip golden brown.

2   Cut a strip of thinly rolled white paste about 18-mm ($\frac{3}{4}$-in) long and 12-mm ($\frac{1}{2}$-in) wide. Shred one long edge finely (like a comb) with scissors or a scalpel to represent stamens. Moisten the plain edge with egg white and wrap around the pistil. Dab a little egg white on to the shredded edges and dip into ground maize or sugartex mixed with a little brown petal dust.

3   Cut out petals by rolling out white paste and cutting with a stephanotis cutter. A small calyx cutter could be used as a substitute. These petals should not be quite as thin as those required for other flowers such as roses and sweet peas. Thin the edges of the petals with a ball tool, then vein and cup them.

4   Insert the wired pistil and stamens through the centre and mould the petals around them.

5   This flower does not have a long

back like jasmine or stephanotis. It sits fairly flat in the calyx. Cut the calyx in pale green-coloured paste with a small star cutter and attach to the base with egg white.

6   The size of the leaves has been reduced as the real leaf is very large and not suitable for use in cake decorating. Make three leaves (*see page 21*) and attach to the flowers as shown.

PANSY

1   Make a circle in the end of a fine wire and bend at right angles. Grease the underside of a polystyrene apple cup or any convex mould with a central hole. Flatten a small ball of flower modelling paste and cover the hole. Push the hooked wire through the paste and secure at the back with a paper clip.

2   Roll some paste out thinly and cut out two petals for the back, two for the sides and one large one for the front. Frill the edges with a cocktail stick (toothpick). The edges will frill better if the board is dusted with a little corn-flour (cornstarch).

3   Place the petals over the dome one at a time, securing each with egg white. Start with the back left, overlap with the back right, then side right followed by side left. Finally add the front petal.

4   Put a tiny piece of yellow-coloured paste in the centre and make a hollow

with a sharp tool. This will press the petals firmly into the ring of wire and will also lift the petals.

5   Cut out two tiny star calyxes in paste. Curve one, pressing a ball tool into the centre. When semi-dry, put egg white on the flat calyx and stick the curved one to it. Put egg white in the centre and slip both on to the back of the flower, the flat side next to it.

6   Paint the shading realistically on the flower when dry.

PERIWINKLE

The periwinkle is a bright mauvy-blue spring flower. The petals are longer and narrower than many blossoms, widening out to a squarish tip.

1   Make a Mexican hat shape in flower modelling paste. Cut out the flower with a small primrose cutter.

2   Use a dogbone modelling tool to stroke the back of the petals firmly from the base to the tip to elongate and thin, keeping a square shape at the tips.

3   Turn the flower over and make a large, straight hole in the centre with a paintbrush handle.

4   Place the flower on a hooked wire and thin the base. Curve the petals back and give a twist to each.

5   Add a yellow-coloured stamen or a tiny piece of yellow-coloured paste to the centre.

6   Paint a narrow white circle around the centre with white blossom tint mixed with edible spirit. The leaves are darkish green and glossy.

POPPY

The poppy does not have a calyx, as the sheath that covers the bud falls off as the petals open.

1   Make a centre by rolling a small piece of green-coloured flower modelling paste into a flat-topped cone. Dip a hooked 26g wire into egg white and press the hook into the base.

2   Roll out a piece of pale golden brown-coloured paste and cut out a disc with a small circular cutter. Stick with egg white to the flat end of the centre.

3   Draw twelve black lines from the centre to the circumference like wheel spokes, or pipe fine lines in black icing. The markings could also be made by pinching with tweezers, the resulting ridges then being painted black with a fine brush. Make black cotton stamens using the same method as for the briar rose (see page 10).

4   Roll out some bright red-coloured paste very thinly and cut out four petals with a poppy cutter or a medium rose petal cutter. If you use the latter, the petals will have to be widened by smoothing well with a ball tool.

5   Press the petals against a veiner or maize husk. Leave over a small domed shape until the petals are partially dry and hold their curves. Dust the base of

each petal with black petal dust.

6   Grease a polystyrene apple cup. Put a small ball of paste in the apple cup and flatten it. Lay the first petal in the cup with the point touching the small disc of paste. Stick with egg white. The second petal is placed opposite with the point overlapping the first petal. Stick with egg white. The third and fourth petals are again placed opposite each other. Push the wired centre through the middle of the petals and secure with egg white. Support the petals in a natural curved shape with small pieces of foam.

PRIMROSE

1 Make a calyx with pale green-coloured flower modelling paste by making a small teardrop shape. Insert a cocktail stick (toothpick) a little way into the narrow end and roll it across the board to hollow and thin. Snip five points at the end with scissors. Push a fine hooked wire through the calyx, keeping the base full.

2 Roll some pale yellow-coloured paste into a Mexican hat shape. Flatten the edge by rolling with a knitting needle. Cut out the flower with a primrose cutter. Press a pointed ridged tool into the centre to make the throat. Thin the petals with a dogbone modelling tool, frill a little more by laying each petal over a finger and rolling a cocktail stick across it.

3 Moisten the calyx with egg white and press the base of the petals into it. Push fine hooked wire through the centre. Push one yellow-coloured stamen into the centre and paint the flower golden yellow at the base of the petals.

ROSE (FULL-BLOWN)

1 Roll a pea-sized piece of yellow-coloured flower modelling paste into a cone. Dip a piece of hooked 24g wire into egg white and push into the base of the cone. Flatten the top. Moisten with egg white and dip into sugartex or maize meal coloured with petal dust.

2 Cut stamen cottons into short lengths, bend them slightly and push into the centre, arranging them around the edge curving inwards.

3 Cut out five medium-sized petals, gently flute the edges and cup with a ball tool. Arrange the petals around the centre, sticking with egg white and overlapping. These petals should curve towards the centre.

4 Using a larger cutter, cut about six more petals, flute and cup. Leave these to dry over a curved object until they hold their shape.

5 Arrange this second layer over the first, but not too tightly. Encourage this layer to curl back slightly. The third layer is constructed in the same way as the second but a larger cutter may be used if desired. Curl these petals well back. Leave to dry.

6 Cut a calyx of an appropriate size. Make a few snips in the sepals. Soften the edges with a ball tool. Moisten the centre with egg white and slip over the wire on to the base of the flower.

ROSE (CECILE BRUNNER)

1 Flatten the top edge of a pea-sized piece of flower modelling paste and roll it out thinly, leaving a thick area at the base.

2 Start rolling diagonally from the top right-hand edge across to the bulbous part.

3 Holding the thick base between your thumb and finger, continue to roll across from right to left; then change to an upward movement so that the bud is tightly rolled and pointed.

4 Make a hook in the end of a 26g wire. Dip into egg white and insert into the base of the bud. Mould the base around the wire, removing any excess paste.

5 Cut out petals with a rose petal cutter. Choose the size of cutter that is about the same length as the bud.

6 Using a dogbone modelling tool, flute the edges of the petals and cup the centres.

7 Moisten the base of a petal with egg white and attach to the centre, keeping the top edge level. Attach two more petals, overlapping each other and evenly spaced. Tuck the edge of the last petal under the first one. The second row has about five petals. Form these as before and attach to the flower, placing the first petal over a join.

8 Roll out a piece of green-coloured paste. Cover with a piece of white paste and roll together. The white side will assume a silvery sheen. Cut out the calyx. Tool the edges with a dogbone modelling tool and make snips in the sepals. Dab egg white in the centre and slip the calyx on to the wire, silvery side next to the rose. Make a teardrop shape in green-coloured paste for the seed pod and put on the wire at the back of the calyx. Neaten the join.

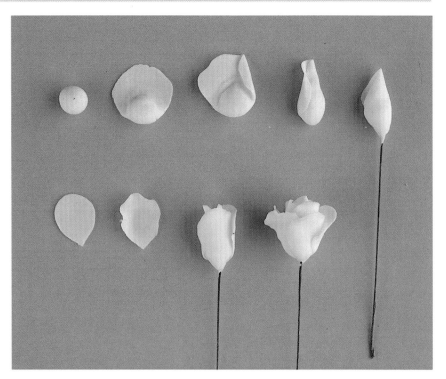

STEPHANOTIS

This fragrant, waxy-looking flower is very popular with brides and useful in bouquets where a medium-sized flower is required. A small calyx cutter could be used if a special stephanotis cutter is not available.

1 Form a pea-sized ball of white flower modelling paste into a Mexican hat shape and roll the edges thinly with a knitting needle. Cut out the flower.

2 Make a throat by pressing a pointed tool into the centre of the flower. Thin the edges of the flower petals and shape from the back with a small ball tool. Indent the front of the petals with a pointed tool.

3 Push a hooked wire through the flower. Shape the back to form a waist under the flower and a fuller base.

4 Roll out some green-coloured paste and cut out the calyx with the smallest star calyx cutter. Dab the centre with egg white and slip over the base of the flower. Shade the back of the flower a creamy green.

SWEET PEA

1 Make a hook in the end of a piece of 26g covered wire. Cover the hook with a small piece of flower modelling paste. Shape like a crescent.

2 Roll out some paste very thinly and cut out a shape with a small rose petal cutter. Cut this shape in half and place the two halves on either side of the centre, the rounded edges in front.

3 Cut out the inner petal which is shaped like a pair of wings. Frill the outside edges with a cocktail stick (toothpick). Brush a line of egg white down the centre of the petal. Place the back of the central bud against this line and fold the petal in half with the centre inside. Open the frilled edge to give a natural apearance.

4 Cut out the large petal. Frill around the outside edge. Make a crease in the middle of this petal and brush egg white along the line. Press the back of the first layer of petals against the crease and fold the large petal around it with the frilled edges even. Open out.

5 Cut out a calyx with the smallest star shape in thinly rolled green-coloured paste. Moisten with egg white and slip over the wire on the base of the flower. Tip back the top edge of the large petal.

6 Make tendrils by cutting a piece of stemfix (flower tape) into four,

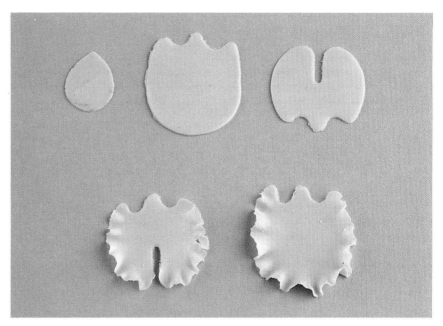

lengthways. Firmly twist a strip around the wire, pulling and twisting until you have a tight thread. Carefully wind this thread round a cocktail stick, leaving a spiral which can then be arranged as you like. Gently bend the flower backwards towards the stem.

7 To make the buds, follow the instructions for the first steps of the flower but instead of cutting a wing-shape, cut

another petal with a rose petal cutter. Soften the edges with a dogbone modelling tool, crease down the middle, brush egg white on the base of the petal and fold around the centre. Pinch back to reinforce the crease. This will have the effect of lifting the front of the petal away from the centre. Add a tiny calyx.

8 Tape several flowers and buds together to make an attractive spray.

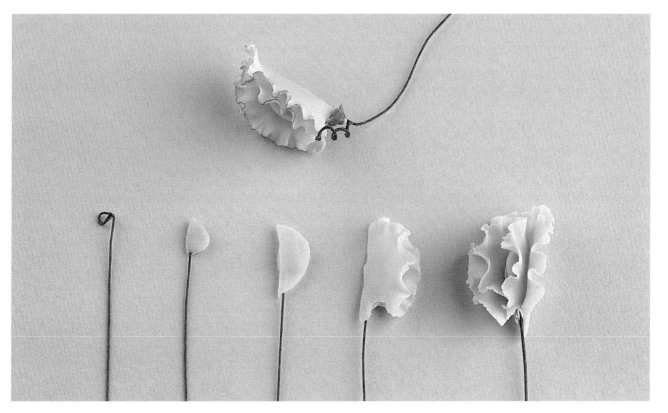

VIOLET

1   Make a small ball of flower modelling paste into a teardrop shape and place the thick end on the tip of a skewer.

2   Cut out five petals, one wider than the others. Continue as for pulled filler blossoms (*see below*).

3   Pinch all the petals between your finger and thumb to flatten. Place each petal in turn over your finger and roll a cocktail stick (toothpick) over it to thin.

4   Push a fine hooked wire through the back of the flower so that the wire stem curves out from the top of the flower. Pinch the edge of the petals to the required shape and arrange so that the wider petal is at the bottom, the two side petals are curved towards the centre and the two top petals stand straight.

5   Insert a deep yellow-coloured stamen in the centre or use a tiny piece of yellow-coloured paste.

6   Paint a green calyx on the back and very fine black lines on the lower petals. Bend the stem so that the head of the flower bends forward.

7   To make the buds, form a small ball of paste into a teardrop shape. Insert a hooked wire into the narrow end. Reshape the point and thin the base by rolling between your fingers. Paint a green calyx on the base.

WHEAT

1   Mould tiny pieces of deep cream-coloured flower modelling paste around the end of a stamen, rolling between the fingers to obtain an oval shape. Mark an indentation down one side with a knife.

Make at least twenty segments for each ear of wheat.

2   Bind the segments to a central wire with fine rose wire and set them in a spiral form to look realistic.

PULLED FILLER BLOSSOMS

These small flowers are very useful, providing interest and lightness in an arrangement of larger flowers. They are not meant to represent any particular flower and are just used for effect.

1   Form a small ball of flower modelling paste into a teardrop shape. Insert a skewer into the paste.

2   Make five cuts with a scalpel. Open out the petals and pinch each one to a point. Press each petal between your finger and thumb to flatten and then pull it into shape. Insert a hooked fine wire moistened with egg white.

3   Make a bud by pushing a hooked wire into a tiny ball of paste. Shape the tip to a point by rolling between your fingers. Thin the base in the same way.

4   Arrange the flowers and buds into a spray or use singly.

LEAVES

GENERAL INSTRUCTIONS

1 Roll green-coloured flower modelling paste out thinly, leaving a thick ridge about 6-mm ($\frac{1}{4}$-in) long. Cut out the required leaf shape.

2 Soften the edges with a dogbone modelling tool. Vein with a plastic veiner or use a mould. Pinch the back of the leaf to emphasize the central vein.

3 Dip a fine covered wire into egg white and insert into the thickened ridge of paste. Press the base of the leaf firmly between your finger and thumb to secure the wire. Dry the leaf over a curved shape to give a natural curl to the edges.

4 For a glossy leaf, paint with gum arabic glaze, or pass quickly in front of steam from a kettle and leave to dry.

PRIMROSE LEAF

This leaf has very distinctive markings which require a mould to reproduce the veinings. As the primrose leaf has a soft structure, a plaster-of-Paris mould is the most successful. It is important to take the impression from the upper surface of the leaf.

MOULDS FOR VEINING

A simple mould can be made by pressing a leaf into quick-drying modelling clay. Remove the leaf when you have obtained a good impression of the veinings and dry the clay, following the manufacturers' instructions.

Clearer markings are obtained by pressing the back of the leaf into the clay but this will result in the leaf veins being raised instead of recessed when an impression is taken from the mould. To obtain a more realistic effect, use plaster of Paris and take an impression of the top surface of the leaf.

To make a plaster-of-Paris mould, roll out a piece of plasticine. Surround with a piece of thin card secured with adhesive tape. Smooth the surface and press in the leaf with the top surface uppermost. Surgical quality plaster of Paris is required to define fine veins. Mix the plaster by pouring the amount of water needed to fill the mould into a bowl. Add plaster by sprinkling over the water until the plaster breaks the surface. Mix quickly with your fingers and pour into the mould. Shake to remove any air bubbles. Leave to set.

When set, remove the cardboard frame, peel away the leaf and leave the mould to dry.

The leaf veins will be standing out from the surface of the plaster so that when the paste is pressed against it, the veins are inset as with a natural leaf.

FLORAL DESIGNS

MORNING GLORY

INGREDIENTS

fruit cake baked in 20-cm (8-in) round cake tin (pan)
boiled, sieved apricot jam
700g (1½lb/3 cups) marzipan
vodka or other alcohol
700g (1½lb/3 cups) sugarpaste
blue food colouring
green food colouring
pink food colouring
yellow food colouring
cornflour (cornstarch)

EQUIPMENT

27.5-cm (11-in) round cake board
rolling pin
pastry brush
sharp knife
greaseproof paper
scriber
No2 paintbrush
adhesive tape
vegetable parchment piping bags
No0 nozzle
No1 nozzle
No2 nozzle
narrow bladed knife or ribbon insert cutter
1 metre (1 yard) deep blue ribbon, 12-mm (½-in) wide
1 metre (1 yard) deep blue ribbon, 6-mm (¼-in) wide
circular Garrett frill cutter
large plain round cutter
cocktail stick (toothpick)

In this cake, two members of the convolvulus family provide the theme of the decoration, with a background of brush embroidery surmounted by a spray of moulded flowers trailing over the side of the cake.

Cover the cake with marzipan and sugarpaste in the usual way. Cover the board with sugarpaste and leave to dry for a few days.

Make a template of the pattern for the brush embroidery and mark the outline on the top of the cake with a scriber. The details can be added later.

Mix small quantities of pale blue- and green-coloured royal icing. Work the brush embroidery, starting with the background leaves and working forward to the blue flowers. When dry, highlight the leaves and flowers with diluted food colourings using a fairly dry paintbrush.

Cut a strip of greaseproof paper of the same length as the circumference of the cake and the same depth. Fold into six sections and cut a deep curve, starting about 12-mm (½-in) from the base. Wrap the strip of paper around the cake and secure with adhesive tape. Mark the scallops around the cake with a scriber.

Pipe a snailstrail around the base of the cake with a No2 nozzle.

Make pairs of slits for ribbon insertion just below the scalloped guideline. Cut short lengths of 6-mm (¼-in) wide ribbon and insert into the slits. Disguise the cuts by piping a fine decoration. With a No0 nozzle and white royal icing, pipe a fine snailstrail over the guideline.

With a No0 nozzle and blue-coloured royal icing, pipe evenly spaced rows of dots below the guideline.

Roll out some sugarpaste very thinly. Cut out with a circular Garrett frill cutter, using a large plain cutter for the centre, producing a frill about 18-mm (¾-in) wide. Roll a cocktail stick (toothpick) back and forth across the scalloped edge. Brush the upper edge of the frill with water and attach just under the ribbon inserts, keeping the points sharply defined. Pipe a neat edge to the top of the frill with a No0 nozzle. Pipe fine decoration between the ribbon inserts with blue-coloured icing.

The bindweed is made in the same way as morning glory (*see page 14*) but the flowers are about half the size. Make some bindweed in white paste, brush the backs of some of the flowers pale pink and dust a line of pink at each of the five evenly spaced creases. Loosely tape together two buds and a leaf, followed by a flower. Continue adding flowers until the trail is of the required length. Entwine bindweed and tiny sprays of white filler blossoms among the morning glory. Cut off the ends of the wires short.

Attach a small cushion of sugarpaste to the cake with a little royal icing and push the ends of the wires into it so that the flowers appear to be coming from the centre of the brush embroidery. Attach a few individual flowers and leaves, facing the opposite direction to those in the spray. Add a large flower with the wire cut off almost completely and stick this into the cushion of paste with a little icing to conceal the ends of the wires underneath.

FLORAL FILIGREE

INGREDIENTS

fruit cake baked in 20-cm (8-in) square cake tin (pan)
boiled, sieved apricot jam
700g (1½lb/3 cups) marzipan
vodka or other alcohol
700g (1½lb/3 cups) royal icing
French pink liquid food colouring

EQUIPMENT

30-cm (12-in) square cake board
rolling pin
pastry brush
sharp knife
greaseproof paper
scriber
vegetable parchment piping bags
No0 nozzle
No1 nozzle
No2 nozzle
medium petal nozzle
waxed paper or plastic wrap
flower nail
cardboard cylinder about 2.5-cm (1-in) diameter
1.25 metres (1⅓ yards) silver edging

Cover the cake with marzipan and position on the board. Then cover the cake with two or three coats of royal icing to achieve a good, smooth surface; for soft cutting, 5ml (1 tsp) glycerine can be added to 450g (1lb/2 cups) royal icing. Coat the exposed edge of the board with royal icing.

Make a template of the side decoration (*see page 80*). Hold against each side of the cake in turn and mark guidelines with a scriber. Pipe random cornelli work on the corners of the cake within the marked lines.

You will need four top collars and four for the board, but it is advisable to make an extra one of each in case of breakage. Make templates from the patterns of the top and board collars and place under uncreased waxed paper or plastic wrap. Glycerine must not be added to royal icing used for collars. Firstly pipe over the flower veins with a No0 nozzle. Then pipe over all the other lines including the borders with a No1 nozzle. Flood the leaves, the large central flower and border of each collar with softened icing.

Using a template made from the pattern, pipe eight leaf motifs in the same way. Dry the leaves in a curved shape over a cardboard cylinder about 2.5-cm (1-in) diameter.

board collar

curved leaf

top collar

For each piped flower, attach a small square of waxed paper to a flower nail with a dot of royal icing. Holding a medium petal nozzle flat against the nail with the thicker edge to the centre, pipe the first petal. Pipe the second petal overlapping the first. Pipe three more petals and neaten with a damp paintbrush if necessary. Using a No1 nozzle and yellow-coloured royal icing, pipe dots for stamens. Leave to dry.

Pipe a line of icing on the board and attach the collars. Pipe a snailstrail with a No2 nozzle around the base of the cake.

Attach the piped flowers in groups to the sides of the cake with dots of royal icing. Pipe an appropriate inscription on the top of the cake.

Use a scriber to mark the centre point on each side of the top edge of the cake. With a No2 nozzle, pipe a line of icing on the top edge of each corner. Position the top collars, taking care to follow the guidelines exactly. Before the icing sets, check that the collars are all level.

Place a curved leaf at each point where the collars join, securing with a little royal icing. Attach the silver edging to the board with dots of royal icing.

CLEMATIS

INGREDIENTS

fruit cake baked in 17.5-cm (7-in) long octagonal cake
*   tin (pan)*
boiled, sieved apricot jam
600g (1¼lb/2½ cups) marzipan
vodka or other alcohol
600g (1¼lb/2½ cups) sugarpaste
assorted food colourings
royal icing
flower modelling paste
egg white

EQUIPMENT

25-cm (10-in) long octagonal cake board
rolling pin
pastry brush
sharp knife
vegetable parchment piping bags
No0 nozzle
No2 nozzle
greaseproof paper
adhesive tape
scriber
paintbrush
dogbone modelling tool
cocktail stick (toothpick)
waxed paper or plastic wrap
2 metres (2¼ yards) mauve satin ribbon, 1.5-mm
*   (1/16-in) wide*

Cover the cake with marzipan and very pale pink-coloured sugarpaste in the usual way. Place in position on the board and using a No2 nozzle, pipe a snailstrail in royal icing around the base of the cake. Leave to dry before attaching a piece of mauve satin ribbon around the cake just above the snailstrail.

Cut a strip of paper of the same length as the circumference of the cake. Wrap the strip around the cake, secure with adhesive tape and mark each corner on the paper. Remove the strip of paper from the cake and using the corner marks as guidelines, draw shallow scallops from one corner to the next for one half of the cake. Then trace this outline through the paper to obtain an identical guideline for the other side. Cut along the scalloped lines and again wrap the strip of paper around the cake, adjusting until the corner marks are correctly aligned. Mark the position for the lace work with a scriber.

Make a template of the clematis design and mark the outline on the top of the cake with a scriber. Follow the brush embroidery technique described on page 7. When the leaves and harebells are complete, make the two clematis flowers which are the focal point of the design. These consist of moulded petals arranged on top of the brush embroidery background.

Make a template of the petal and cut out eight for each clematis. Alternatively, you can use a cutter of similar shape. Cup each petal slightly by working the centre with a dogbone modelling tool and gently flute by rolling a cocktail stick (toothpick) across the edges. Leave to set over a curved shape.

When dry, stick the petals in position with egg white. Pipe in the centres and stamens with a No1 nozzle and yellow-coloured royal icing. Paint the shading with diluted food colouring and add a touch of burgundy to the tips of the stamens.

Using a No0 nozzle, pipe lace pieces in the form of tiny bows on to non-stick film. Leave to dry thoroughly before attaching all round the cake with dots of royal icing, following the scribed guidelines. Make little bows in the remaining mauve ribbon and attach to the sides of the cake as shown.

pattern for clematis petal

DAFFODIL EASTER CAKE

INGREDIENTS

fruit cake baked in 20-cm (8-in) round cake tin (pan)
boiled, sieved apricot jam
700g (1½lb/3 cups) marzipan
vodka or other alcohol
700g (1½lb/3 cups) royal icing
brown liquid food colouring
black liquid food colouring
egg yellow liquid food colouring
leaf green liquid food colouring
lemon liquid food colouring

EQUIPMENT

30-cm (12-in) round cake board
rolling pin
pastry brush
sharp knife
tracing paper
waxed paper or plastic wrap
vegetable parchment piping bags
No0 nozzle
No1 nozzle
No2 nozzle
paintbrush
scriber
*2 metres (2¼ yards) willow green satin ribbon, 3-mm
   (⅛-in) wide*
*2 metres (2¼ yards) baby maize satin ribbon, 3-mm
   (⅛-in) wide*
*2 metres (2¼ yards) dark brown satin ribbon, 3-mm
   (⅛-in) wide*

The royal icing used for the collar should not contain glycerine.

Cover the cake with marzipan and leave to dry for a few days before sticking to the board with a little apricot jam. Mix a little lemon liquid food colouring into some royal icing; to achieve a soft cutting texture, 5ml (1 tsp) glycerine can be added for 450g (1lb) of icing. Cover the cake with two coats of icing. Also coat the exposed edge of the board.

Make a template of the collar and stick firmly to a large board. Cover with uncreased waxed paper or plastic wrap and secure with dots of royal icing or masking tape.

With pale yellow-coloured icing and a No0 nozzle, pipe filigree in the open spaces using 'S' shapes, all of which must touch each other at some point. Then outline the daffodils and leaves with a No1 nozzle and dark brown-coloured royal icing (to which a little black liquid food colouring has been added). Use a damp paintbrush to neaten any uneven joins. Outline the lettering and the borders with a No1 nozzle and white royal icing.

Half-fill piping bags with white, bright yellow-coloured and green-coloured icing of flooding consistency and snip holes in the ends about the size of a No2 nozzle. Carefully flood the leaves green, taking care not to obscure the brown outlines. Use a damp brush to coax the icing into any awkward little corners. Using yellow-coloured icing, flood the flower heads. Complete by flooding the outside bands of the collar and the lettering with white royal icing. Dry quickly in a warm place, such as under a desk lamp to obtain a good sheen.

Make a board template by tracing only the plain border around the edge of the top collar, not the flowers or lettering. Cut out a circle from the centre so that the template will easily slip over the cake on to the board. Mark a line around the outer edge of the template with a scriber. Remove the template and pipe a circle following the guideline with white royal icing and a No1 nozzle. Pipe another line within the first, making a band about 5-mm (¼-in) wide. With a No0 nozzle and pale yellow-coloured icing, pipe random filigree between the cake and the inner circle. With white icing, flood the band.

Stick bands of ribbon to the edge of the board and around the base of the cake as illustrated.

Remove the collar from the waxed paper by sliding it to the edge of a table until a small part overhangs. Gently peel off the waxed paper, rotating until all the paper has been removed. With a No2 nozzle, pipe a ring of royal icing around the top edge of the cake and supporting the collar carefully with both hands, place in position on the cake.

See overleaf for collar pattern

33

TYROLEAN-STYLE EMBROIDERED CAKE

INGREDIENTS
fruit cake baked in 20-cm (8-in) square cake tin (pan)
boiled, sieved apricot jam
700g (1½lb/3 cups) marzipan
vodka or other alcohol
700g (1½lb/3 cups) royal icing
assorted food colourings

EQUIPMENT
27.5-cm (11-in) square cake board
rolling pin
pastry brush
sharp knife
greaseproof paper
scriber
vegetable parchment piping bags
No0 nozzle
No1 nozzle
No2 nozzle

Cover the cake with marzipan and leave to dry for a few days before sticking to the board with a little apricot jam. Then cover with two coats of royal icing. Also coat the exposed edge of the board.

Pipe a neat snailstrail in white royal icing around the base of the cake with a No2 nozzle.

Make a template of the scalloped edge and the embroidery and mark the main features on all four sides of the cake with a scriber. The smaller details can easily be filled in freehand. Mark matching scallops around the top of the cake. Make a template of the floral motifs for the top of the cake and mark the outlines with a scriber.

Using a No0 nozzle, pipe random cornelli work in white royal icing within the scalloped top border. Finish the inner and outer edges with a neat row of shells piped with a No1 nozzle.

Using either No0 or No1 nozzles, half-fill piping bags with the different coloured icings required for the floral design. Work the larger flowers in satin stitch, and the small flowers and leaves in lazy daisy stitch (*see page 7*). Hold the nozzle close to the surface of the cake and pipe over the outlines. Pipe in stamens when the flowers are dry.

Pipe a greeting in a dark-coloured royal icing with a No1 nozzle on the top of the cake.

ROSES AND LILY-OF-THE-VALLEY

INGREDIENTS

fruit cake baked in 17.5-cm (7-in) round cake tin (pan)
boiled, sieved apricot jam
600g (1¼lb/2½ cups) marzipan
vodka or other alcohol
600g (1¼lb/2½ cups) sugarpaste
225g (8oz/1 cup) extension work royal icing (adding 1ml (¼ tsp) liquid glucose and a pinch of gum arabic)
pink blossom tint
moulded roses
lily-of-the-valley
leaves

EQUIPMENT

25-cm (10-in) round cake board
rolling pin
pastry brush
sharp knife
scriber
paintbrush
1.1 metres (1¼ yards) pale pink satin ribbon, 1.5-mm (1/16-in) wide
loops made from 1.5-mm (1/16-in) wide white ribbon
greaseproof paper
vegetable parchment piping bags
No0 nozzle
No1 nozzle
piece of perspex (plexiglas) or a smooth board
tilting turntable

Cover the cake with marzipan and sugarpaste in the usual way. Cover the board with sugarpaste and leave to dry. Place the cake on the board.

Mark a circle about 6-mm (¼-in) from the base of the cake, taking care to make this line as faint as possible so that it will hardly show when the cake is completed. Divide this circle into sections about 3.75-cm (1½-in) wide. Mark a line around the cake about 3-cm (1¼-in) from the base and colour this area pink by mixing pink blossom tint with vodka or gin and brushing on evenly with a soft paintbrush. Attach a length of pink ribbon on the top line and another length to the base of the cake.

Cut a strip of greaseproof paper of the same length as the circumference of the cake and of the same depth. Fold into even sections about 3.75-cm (1½-in) wide. Cut the top edges into scallops. Unfold the strip and attach to the cake. Mark the positions of the scallops for the embroidered top border.

Cut a circle of greaseproof paper 3.75-cm (1½-in) less than the diameter of the iced cake, lay on the top of the cake and mark around this with a scriber, to form a border.

The base of the extension work consists of loops piped when the cake is in an upside-down position. It is essential that the icing is left to harden on the cake for a few days before starting the extension work.

Place a piece of perspex or a smooth board on top of the cake, invert the cake and board and place upside-down on a tilting turntable.

With a No1 nozzle and white extension work royal icing, pipe dropped loops of even size, suspended from the board at the marked points. Leave to dry for several hours before turning the cake back to the correct position. Tilting the turntable towards you, pipe the vertical lines of the extension work with a No0 nozzle from the ribbon down to the arches. Attach the threads of icing very carefully to the loops so that they do not break. Remove any surplus icing with a damp paintbrush.

When dry, pipe hailspots on the extension work and a floral embroidered border around the scribed line on top of the cake, following the pattern.

Make a small spray of roses, lily-of-the-valley and white ribbon loops and place in the centre of the cake.

pattern for floral top border

PETAL CAKE

INGREDIENTS

fruit cake baked in 20-cm (8-in) petal-shaped cake tin
*   *(pan)*
boiled, sieved apricot jam
700g (1½lb/3 cups) marzipan
vodka or other alcohol
700g (1¼lb/3 cups) sugarpaste
royal icing
modelling paste
violets
yellow roses and leaves
small filler blossoms

EQUIPMENT

27.5-cm (11-in) round cake board
rolling pin
pastry brush
sharp knife
2 metres (2¼ yards) yellow satin ribbon, 1.5-mm
*   *(1/16-in) wide*
1 metre (1 yard) yellow satin ribbon, 3-mm (1/8-in)
*   *wide*
greaseproof paper
scriber
vegetable parchment piping bags
No0 nozzle
No1 nozzle
small piece of bridal tulle
domed shape
plastic wrap

Cover the cake with marzipan and sugarpaste in the usual way. Position the cake on the board. Attach 3-mm (1/8-in) wide yellow ribbon to the edge of the board with a little royal icing.

Cut a piece of greaseproof paper of the same depth as the cake and the same width as one of the petals. Draw a curved line diagonally from the top left-hand corner to the bottom right-hand corner and cut along this line. Hold the piece of paper against the side of the cake and use a scriber to mark the curved line in each petal.

Cut six pieces of 1.5-mm (1/16-in) wide yellow satin ribbon to fit this curve. Using a No0 nozzle, pipe fine lines of royal icing over the guidelines and attach the pieces of ribbon in each petal.

Pipe a snailstrail around the base of the cake in royal icing with a No1 nozzle.

Make a template of the design for the lace pieces and cover with waxed paper or plastic wrap. With a No0 nozzle pipe over the outline. When dry, attach the lace pieces with small dots of royal icing on both sides of the pieces of yellow ribbon. Pipe embroidery on the sides of the cake with a No0 nozzle.

Make a template of the parasol pattern. Place on a piece of tulle and cut round the outline neatly. Attach the teetemplate to a domed shape with a little royal icing and cover with plastic wrap. Hold the tulle shape over the template and secure by piping the lines of the parasol frame in yellow-coloured royal icing with a No0 nozzle. Pipe around the outline, coaxing it to follow the domed shape closely. Pipe decorative work in white royal icing between the lines of the frame. Leave the parasol to dry on the dome. Make a handle by rolling a little modelling paste into a long slender shape. Leave to dry. Then tie a length of 1.5-mm (1/16-in) wide ribbon around the handle.

Position the parasol on top of the cake, securing it with a little royal icing. Insert a small cushion of sugarpaste to hold the violets just inside the parasol. Cut the flower wires short and stick them into the sugarpaste to make a neat arrangement. Then insert the handle of the parasol. Make a ribbon bow with trailing ends and attach to the end of the handle with royal icing.

Pipe the recipient's name in yellow-coloured royal icing on the top of the cake.

Stick small pieces of sugarpaste on the cake board between each petal and arrange small posies by sticking the short wire ends into the paste.

FLORAL COLLAR

INGREDIENTS

fruit cake baked in 20-cm (8-in) round cake tin (pan)
boiled, sieved apricot jam
700g (1½lb/3 cups) marzipan
vodka or other alcohol
700g (1½lb/3 cups) royal icing
black food colouring
sugarpaste
6 moulded leaves (not wired)
1 full-blown moulded rose

EQUIPMENT

30-cm (12-in) round cake board
rolling pin
pastry brush
sharp knife
greaseproof paper
waxed paper or plastic wrap
vegetable parchment piping bags
No0 nozzle
No1 nozzle
paintbrush
scriber
tilting turntable
1½ metres (1½ yards) moss green satin ribbon, 3-mm
(⅛-in) wide

For flood work, the royal icing should not contain glycerine. It should be soft enough to settle with a smooth surface but not so soft that it runs over the outlines.

Cover the cake with marzipan and leave to dry for a few days before sticking to the board with a little apricot jam. Then cover with two coats of pale moss green-coloured royal icing. Also coat the exposed edge of the board.

Make a template of the collar and stick firmly to a large board. Cover with uncreased waxed paper or plastic wrap and secure with dots of icing or masking tape. Outline the design with a No1 nozzle and white royal icing. Add a little water to some more white royal icing and half-fill a large piping bag without a nozzle. Snip a hole in the end about the size of a No2 writing nozzle. Flood the outside areas of the flowers and leaves, then the border of the collar, using a damp paintbrush to coax the icing into any awkward little corners. Dry quickly in a warm place, such as under a desk lamp.

Using templates of the flower and leaf motif, follow the same procedure to prepare the required number to decorate the cake board.

Make a template of the spray. Mark six equidistant positions on the side of the cake. Either use a tilting turntable or wedge the cake board at an angle. Then scribe the outline of the spray in the six marked positions. Outline the first spray with a No0 nozzle in white royal icing and then flood as above. Continue in this way until all the flower sprays are completed.

Pipe a neat border around the base with a No2 nozzle.

Remove the flower and leaf motifs from the waxed paper and arrange on the board at regular intervals.

Tie moss green ribbon around the base of the cake just above the border, finishing with a double bow.

Remove the collar from the waxed paper by sliding it to the edge of a table until a small part overhangs. Gently peel off the waxed paper, rotating the collar until all the paper has been removed. With a No2 nozzle, pipe a ring of royal icing around the top edge of the cake and, supporting the collar carefully with both hands, place in position on the cake.

Arrange the moulded rose leaves attractively in the centre of the top of the cake, securing with a little royal icing. Attach a small piece of sugarpaste in the centre of the leaves, cut off the wire from the rose very short and press into the sugarpaste, securing with a little royal icing.

See overleaf
for collar pattern

FLORAL EMBROIDERY

INGREDIENTS

fruit cake baked in 17.5-cm (7-in) square cake tin (pan)
boiled, sieved apricot jam
600g (1¼lb/2½ cups) marzipan
vodka or other alcohol
600g (1¼lb/2½ cups) sugarpaste
brown food colouring
leaf green food colouring
lemon food colouring
moss green food colouring
paprika food colouring

EQUIPMENT

25-cm (10-in) square cake board
rolling pin
pastry brush
sharp knife
greaseproof paper
vegetable parchment piping bags
No1 nozzle
No2 nozzle
paint brush
1 metre (1 yard) cream satin ribbon, 6-mm (¼-in) wide
1.1 metres (1¼ yards) cream satin ribbon, 12-mm (½-in) wide

The floral design on this cake represents a simple form of crewel work, a type of embroidery which is worked in wool on a coarse background. Only three 'stitches' have been used in the decoration: long and short, satin and French knots (*see page 7*).

Cover the cake with marzipan and sugarpaste in the usual way. Coat the board if wished. Place the cake on the board and leave to dry for about two days.

Enlarge or reduce the flower design to a suitable size for the cake. The easiest way of doing this accurately is to use a photocopier.

Make a template of the pattern for the large flower heads and mark the outline on the cake with a scriber; also mark the outlines of the leaves. Transfer the flower and leaf design to the sides of the cake, where required, to make a balanced design. The stems can be piped in later to join up the floral motifs.

Mix all the colours required for the design and half-fill small piping bags containing No1 nozzles. Starting with the background, pipe in the embroidery. Pipe a neat border around the base of the cake with a No2 nozzle.

Attach 6-mm (¼-in) wide cream ribbon to the base of the cake and 12-mm (½-in) wide ribbon to the edge of the board.

Pipe an appropriate inscription.

See overleaf for embroidery pattern

SPRING FLOWER ARRANGEMENT

INGREDIENTS

fruit or Madeira cake baked in a small loaf tin (pan)
    about 17.5 × 7.5-cm ((7 × 3-in)
boiled, sieved apricot jam
450g (1lb/2 cups) marzipan
vodka or other alcohol
450g (1lb/2 cups) sugarpaste
brown food colouring
French pink food colouring
cocoa powder or brown blossom tint
black blossom tint
green blossom tint
periwinkles
primroses
Christmas roses
flowering currant
leaves

EQUIPMENT

25-cm (10-in) rectangular cake board
rolling pin
pastry brush
sharp knife
modelling tools
cocktail stick (toothpick)
fine florist's wires
brown florist's tape
fine wooden skewer
plastic drinking straws or holders

The base of this spring flower arrangement is a cake masquerading as a piece of bark. This is a design that will appeal to decorators who love modelling and hate piping! Marzipan would be a very effective alternative to sugarpaste as it also colours and models well.

Cut off all the corners and sharp edges from the cake. If using sugarpaste, apply the marzipan in the usual way. Colour the sugarpaste a very light brown, which makes a good base colour; the shading is achieved by brushing with edible powder colour. Cocoa powder is preferable to brown blossom tint because of its flavour. Brush the marzipan with vodka and apply the sugarpaste thickly and roughly, making no attempt to achieve a smooth finish.

If using marzipan only, colour this light brown and mould it around the cake with your hands, forming hollows and raising other areas by pinching to obtain a rough log shape. Score deep grooves and hollows with modelling tools. For greater realism, study a piece of real bark or consult a nature reference book.

Cover the outside edge of the board and stipple with brown and green blossom tint. Position the cake and brush the bark with cocoa powder or brown blossom tint, with a touch of black to emphasize the hollows. Add a touch of green blossom tint here and there to represent moss.

The flowering currant is made of tiny pulled flowers. A cocktail stick (toothpick) is used instead of the usual wooden skewer. Cut five petals in sugarpaste and insert a stamen instead of a hooked wire for each bloom. When dry, clusters of these tiny flowers are bound on to a fine wire with a few buds. Use brown florist's tape to join clusters of flowers and leaves to form a bunch.

Plan how you wish to arrange the flowers. Add an extra cushion of brown-coloured sugarpaste to the areas where the clusters of flowers are to be arranged. Trim the wires of the smaller flowers and leaves closely and push ends into the sugarpaste. (The wires must be short enough to be contained in this extra sugarpaste and not penetrate the actual cake for reasons of food hygiene.) For the longer-stemmed twigs, make holes in the appropriate places with a fine wooden skewer. Insert a short drinking straw, which has the end plugged with icing. Feed the wire into the straw so that it does not touch the cake. Special plastic holders for this purpose are available.

ROSE AND HAREBELLS

INGREDIENTS

fruit cake baked in 20-cm (8-in) long octagonal cake tin (pan)
boiled, sieved apricot jam
700g (1½lb/3 cups) marzipan
vodka or other alcohol
700g (1½lb/3 cups) sugarpaste
royal icing
flower modelling paste
assorted food colourings
1 full-blown rose
1 rosebud
5 rose leaves
3 sprays of harebells

EQUIPMENT

25-cm (10-in) long octagonal cake board
rolling pin
pastry brush
sharp knife
vegetable parchment piping bags
No0 nozzle
No1 nozzle
tracing paper
scriber
paintbrush
waxed paper or plastic wrap

Cover the cake with marzipan and sugarpaste in the usual way. Place in position on the board. With a No1 nozzle, pipe a snailstrail in white royal icing around the base of the cake.

Make a template of the rose and harebells and mark the outline on the top of the cake with a scriber. Execute the design in brush embroidery (*see page 7*). Pipe the recipient's name or other inscription to the right of the flowers.

Make a template of the small spray, mark the outline on the four short panels and pipe embroidery following the colours shown in the photograph.

Attach a small piece of sugarpaste to the board at the front of the cake and stick the short wires of the moulded flowers and leaves into this, not the cake.

With a No0 nozzle, pipe lace pieces on waxed paper or plastic wrap. Leave to dry before attaching to the cake with dots of royal icing.

POPPIES

INGREDIENTS

fruit cake baked in 20-cm (8-in) round cake tin (pan)
boiled, sieved apricot jam
700g (1½lb/3 cups) marzipan
vodka or other alcohol
700g (1½lb/3 cups) sugarpaste
royal icing
4 moulded poppies
2 ears of wheat
4 leaves

EQUIPMENT

27.5-cm (11-in) round cake board
rolling pin
pastry brush
sharp knife
vegetable parchment piping bags
No0 nozzle
No1 nozzle
No2 nozzle
greaseproof paper
No2 sable paintbrush
75cm (¾ yard) scarlet satin ribbon, 1.5-mm (1/16-in) wide

Cover the cake with marzipan and cream-coloured sugarpaste in the usual way. The shade of the sugarpaste is achieved by using egg yellow food colouring and a trace of brown. Knead well to distribute the colour evenly. Cover the board with cream-coloured sugarpaste. Leave to dry.

Position the cake on the board. Pipe a snailstrail around the base of the cake, using deep cream-coloured royal icing and a No2 nozzle.

Make a template of the poppy design and position it so that the stalks are touching the side of the cake. Mark the outline with a scriber. Paint the background very softly with food colourings, adding more definition as you work towards the edge of the cake. Using a No0 nozzle, work the poppy spray in brush embroidery. This creates an effect of poppies in a field receding into the distance.

Place a small pad of sugarpaste on the board and arrange the moulded poppies, ears of wheat and leaves decoratively, securing the wired ends in the sugarpaste.

Mark the positions on the side of the cake for the ears of wheat. Using a No2 nozzle and deep cream-coloured royal icing, pipe bulbs in pairs as shown in the diagram, drawing each one to a point at the side. Continue until each ear is the required length, and then pipe another row of bulbs along the centre of the lines. Pipe the stalks, using a No1 nozzle. Leave to dry. Tie tiny bows of red ribbon and attach between the stalks and ears of wheat, as shown in the diagram.

VALENTINE CAKE

INGREDIENTS

fruit cake baked in 20-cm (8-in) heart-shaped cake tin (pan)
boiled, sieved apricot jam
700g (1½lb/3 cups) marzipan
vodka or other alcohol
700g (1¼lb/3 cups) sugarpaste
royal icing
violet food colouring
flower modelling paste
4 large sweet peas
4 leaves
12 sprays purple and white filler blossoms

EQUIPMENT

25-cm (10-in) heart-shaped cake board
pastry brush
rolling pin
sharp knife or scalpel
greaseproof paper
adhesive tape
scriber
vegetable parchment piping bags
No0 nozzle
No1 nozzle
cocktail stick (toothpick)
ribbon insert cutter or fine pointed knife
50cm (½ yard) white ribbon, 1.5-mm (1/16-in) wide
mauve ribbon loops and trails
posy holder

Cover the cake with marzipan and sugarpaste in the usual way. Place the cake on the board. Pipe a snailstrail in white royal icing around the base with a No1 nozzle.

Cut a strip of greaseproof paper of the same length and depth as the side of the cake. Make a template of the pattern for the side line-work and trace on to the strip of greaseproof paper, repeating as necessary to form a continuous line. Wrap the strip around the cake and secure with adhesive tape. Mark the line for the graduated loops with a scriber.

Using a No0 nozzle and violet-coloured royal icing, pipe lines and dots following the scribed line. Pipe embroidery in each section in white royal icing.

Make a template of the heart shape and place on a small piece of mauve-coloured flower modelling paste rolled out very thinly. Cut out the shape with a sharp knife or scalpel. With a cocktail stick (toothpick), frill the edge of the heart by rotating the stick backwards and forwards to stretch the edge. Lay the heart in the centre of the top of the cake.

Using a ribbon insert cutter or a fine pointed knife, cut slits at intervals around the edge of the heart just inside the frill. Insert small pieces of ribbon. Tie a neat bow with trailing ends and attach to the heart with a little royal icing.

The lovebirds can be made from sugarpaste using the bas relief technique or by figure piping. Attach the birds to the heart with a little royal icing.

Make an arrangement of sweet peas and filler blossoms, adding a few leaves and ribbon loops. Insert a posy holder into the cake. The wires of the spray should be pushed into the holder, not directly into the cake. A few flowers may also be arranged on the board.

pattern for side line-work

INGREDIENTS

Genoese or Victoria sponge baked in 20-cm (8-in)
round cake tin (pan)
boiled, sieved apricot jam
300g (10oz/1¼ cups) buttercream
10ml (2tsp) instant coffee granules dissolved in 20ml
(4tsp) hot water
black food colouring
green food colouring
orange food colouring
yellow food colouring

EQUIPMENT

27.5-cm (11-in) round cake board
pastry brush
sharp knife
serrated scraper
greaseproof paper
two 20-cm (8-in) round pieces of cardboard or thin
cake boards
waxed paper or plastic wrap
vegetable parchment piping bags
No1 nozzle
No2 nozzle
No8 star nozzle
basketwork nozzle

Stir the cool coffee into the buttercream and reserve about half. Cut the cake in half and sandwich together with jam or buttercream. Brush the cake all over with apricot jam and place on the board.

Coat the sides of the cake with coffee-coloured buttercream. Use a serrated scraper to smooth and texture the sides, as shown.

Make a template of the lilies and lay this on one of the pieces of cardboard in the desired position. Cover with uncreased waxed paper or plastic wrap.

Mix about 90g (3oz) of the reserved buttercream with dark brown food colouring, adding a little black to deepen it further. With a No1 nozzle, pipe over all the outlines of the flowers and leaves. Overpipe all the lines to add depth.

Half-fill three small piping bags with green-, orange- and yellow-coloured buttercream and cut small holes in the ends of the bags. Fill in each section of the design with the appropriate colour, taking care not to cover the dark outlines.

Half-fill a large piping bag with coffee-coloured buttercream, cut a slightly larger hole in the end and fill in the background, leaving no gaps and piping right up to the outlines. Then, with a basketwork nozzle in a large piping bag, pipe straight lines in coffee-coloured buttercream from the top to the bottom of the design, working across until the whole area is completely covered. This side will form the back of the design.

Place a piece of waxed paper or plastic wrap on top of the design and cover with the second piece of cardboard. Turn over so that the bottom piece of cardboard is on top. Remove it, exposing the design which should still be covered with the waxed paper or plastic wrap. Examine the surface carefully. Prick any air bubbles with a pin and rub the area gently through the waxed paper to smooth out any holes. Replace the piece of cardboard and press the cardboard together gently to make the buttercream surface flat and even. Freeze until quite hard.

When ready to use, remove the bottom piece of cardboard and the waxed paper or plastic wrap. Lay the design in position on the cake and remove the remaining cardboard and waxed paper or plastic wrap. Allow to thaw, then trim the edges and pipe decorative borders around the top and base of the cake with a No8 star nozzle and dark brown-coloured buttercream.

CHRISTMAS BOX

INGREDIENTS

fruit cake baked in 20-cm (8-in) square cake tin (pan)
boiled, sieved apricot jam
700g (1½lb/3 cups) marzipan
vodka or other alcohol
700g (1¼lb/3 cups) sugarpaste
green food colouring
black food colouring
egg white
green-coloured royal icing
25g (1oz/2 tbsp) modelling paste
Christmas roses
holly leaves
mistletoe

EQUIPMENT

27.5-cm (11-in) square cake board
rolling pin
pastry brush
sharp knife
tracing wheel
scriber
paintbrush
holly leaf cutter
vegetable parchment piping bag
No2 nozzle
No4 nozzle
1 metre (1 yard) red ribbon, 12-mm (½-in) wide
1 metre (1 yard) red ribbon, 6-mm (¼-in) wide

Cover the cake with marzipan, leaving sharp corners as for royal icing. Colour 450g (1lb/2 cups) of the sugarpaste with green food colouring, adding a touch of black to make a deep shade. Cover the cake board with the same green-coloured sugarpaste.

Moisten the sides of the cake with the chosen alcohol. Cut strips of green-coloured sugarpaste of the same size as the sides of the cake. Attach to the cake, neatening the corners. Use a tracing wheel to mark a decorative line on both sides of each corner.

Cut out a square 5-cm (2-in) larger than the cake in the white sugarpaste. Mark a border 2.5-cm (1-in) all round the square. Cut out pieces from each corner as shown. Lift the cut piece of sugarpaste on to the cake – do not moisten it. Position it carefully so that the corners match and fold over the edges to form a neat lid. Moisten the edges with a damp paintbrush and stick down. Decorate the edge of the lid with a line made by a tracing wheel.

Cut out tiny holly leaves with a cutter in the remaining deep green-coloured sugarpaste. Cut out holly berries in red-coloured sugarpaste with the tip of a No4 nozzle. Arrange the leaves and berries on the lid securing with egg white.

Using a No2 nozzle, pipe a neat border around the base of the cake in green-coloured royal icing. Stick the 12-mm (½-in) wide red ribbon in place, as shown.

Make a template for the label, cut out in modelling paste and leave to dry flat. Pipe a decorative border and an inscription in green-coloured royal icing. Thread a short piece of 6-mm (¼-in) wide red ribbon through the hole.

Make the remaining 6-mm (¼-in) wide ribbon into loops and arrange with Christmas roses, holly and mistletoe to cover the point where the ribbon crosses, sticking the short wires into a small cushion of sugarpaste. Tuck the label under the edge of the arrangement.

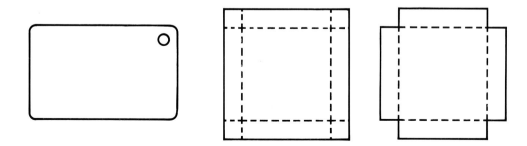

PANSIES

INGREDIENTS
*fruit cake baked in a 20-cm (8-in) round cake tin
 (pan)*
boiled, sieved apricot jam
700g (1½lb/3 cups) marzipan
vodka or other alcohol
700g (1½lb/3 cups) sugarpaste
pansies
filler blossoms

EQUIPMENT
27.5-cm (11-in) round cake board
rolling pin
pastry brush
sharp knife
greaseproof paper
adhesive tape
scriber
vegetable parchment piping bags
No0 nozzle
No1 nozzle
circular Garrett frill cutter
cocktail stick (toothpick)
paintbrush
florist's tape
wooden skewer
plastic drinking straw or holder

Cover the cake with marzipan and sugarpaste in the usual way. Leave for 24 hours.

Cut a strip of paper of the same length as the circumference of the cake and about 4-cm (1½-in) deep. Fold into six to eight sections and cut a curve in the top edge to form the line of the frill. Unfold the strip of paper and wrap around the sides of the cake, securing with headed pins. Mark the position of the frill with a scriber. Pipe a snailstrail in royal icing around the base of the cake with a No1 nozzle.

Make a template of the pattern of the embroidery and mark the outline on the side of the cake with a scriber. Complete the design, using the brush embroidery technique.

To make the frill, cut out circles of thinly rolled sugarpaste with a Garrett frill cutter and cut holes in the centres. Open out each circle and frill one edge by rolling a cocktail stick (toothpick) back and forth to stretch the sugarpaste; this will give the frill the necessary fullness.

Using a damp paintbrush, moisten the line where scribed and attach the frill, cutting it at the top point of the scallop. Repeat with another circle of sugarpaste, turning under the edge which overlaps the first section of frill and attaching it in the same way. Neaten the join between each section. Pipe a decorative edge over the top line of the frill to conceal the join.

Make a hole with a wooden skewer in a suitable position on top of the cake. Insert a piece of wide drinking straw which has the end plugged with icing.

Tape brightly coloured pansies and filler blossoms into a spray and feed the wires into the straw so that they do not touch the cake. Special plastic holders for this purpose are available.

ORCHIDS

INGREDIENTS

fruit cake baked in 25-cm (10-in) hexagonal cake tin (pan)
boiled, sieved apricot jam
900g (2lb/3½ cups) marzipan
vodka or other alcohol
900g (2lb/3½ cups) sugarpaste
lemon food colouring
paprika food colouring
extension work royal icing (see page 36)
flower modelling paste
cornflour (cornstarch)
orchids
orange blossom
roses

EQUIPMENT

35-cm (14-in) hexagonal cake board
greaseproof paper
scriber
vegetable parchment piping bags
No00 nozzle
No0 nozzle
No1 nozzle
circular Garrett frill cutter
5-cm (2-in) diameter plain cutter
paintbrush
cocktail stick (toothpick)

This cake would be suitable for a more mature bride or perhaps for a second wedding. The design could be adapted for a tiered cake.

Cover the cake with marzipan in the usual way. Colour some sugarpaste with paprika food colouring and a little lemon food colouring to make a delicate apricot shade. Cover the cake with sugarpaste. When dry, place on the board.

Make a template of the three-tiered extension work and scribe the outline on to the sides of the cake.

Pipe a snailstrail in royal icing around the base of the cake with a No0 nozzle.

Pipe six to eight rows of bridgework all around the base of the cake with a No0 or No1 nozzle, allowing each row to dry before piping the next row exactly on top of the previous one.

Pipe the vertical extension work with a No00 or No0 nozzle by touching the nozzle to the guideline immediately above the bridge, squeezing out a thread of icing smoothly and attaching it by drawing the nozzle down past the bridge, releasing the pressure when you reach the bridge. Neaten off any little tails by drawing a damp paintbrush under the bridge. The threads should be piped so close together that there would be no space to insert another thread. Pipe extension work all around the base of the cake, taking care to ensure that it remains vertical.

Pipe a second row of bridgework in the same way, following the guideline above the first row. Then pipe vertical extension work as before, keeping within the diagonal guidelines. Pipe another bridge above this and more vertical extension work to form the points. Leave to dry.

The frill is made from an equal mixture of flower modelling paste and sugarpaste. This combination can be rolled out very thinly for a delicate effect. Colour the mixture similarly to the cake but a little darker. Cut out a circle of paste with a frill cutter. Cut the centre out with a 5-cm (2-in) plain cutter, giving a very narrow frill. Open out and frill in the usual way on a surface dusted with cornflour (cornstarch). Use a paintbrush to moisten a line just above the extension work and attach the frill.

Cut a 20-cm (8-in) circle of greaseproof paper and lay on the top of the cake. Mark a guideline around the edge with a scriber and pipe embroidery over this.

Make a very loose, informal spray of orchids, orange blossom and roses, and arrange on the cake by inserting the ends of the wires into a plastic holder which can be pushed into the cake. Alternatively, the spray can be laid on the cake in situ, in which case it will not be necessary to secure it. The long ends of the spray should be arranged so that they trail over the side above the lowest point of the extension work.

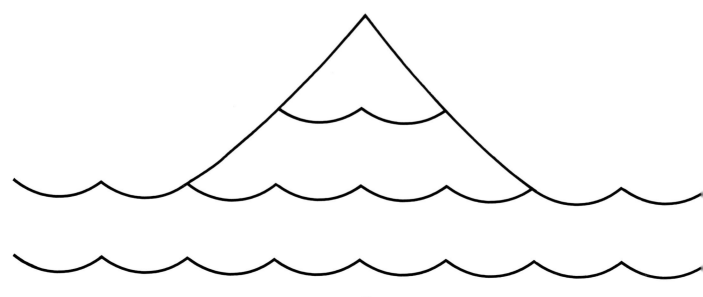

EASTER DAISIES

INGREDIENTS

fruit cake baked in 20-cm (8-in) hexagonal cake tin (pan)
boiled, sieved apricot jam
700g (1½lb/3 cups) marzipan
vodka or other alcohol
700g (1½lb/3 cups) sugarpaste
royal icing
assorted food colourings

EQUIPMENT

27.5-cm (11-in) hexagonal cake board
rolling pin
pastry brush
sharp knife
1.25 metres (1⅓ yards) blue satin ribbon, 6-mm (¼-in) wide
greaseproof paper
waxed paper or plastic wrap
vegetable parchment piping bags
No2 nozzle
daisy cutter
small blossom cutter

Cover the cake with marzipan and pale blue-coloured sugarpaste in the usual way. Cover the board with pale blue-coloured sugarpaste and leave to dry. Position the cake on the board. Attach the blue ribbon around the base of the cake, securing with royal icing.

Make a template from the pattern and cover with uncreased waxed paper or plastic wrap. Half-fill piping bags with white and yellow-coloured royal icing and cut small holes in the ends of both bags. Complete the design using the figure piping technique. Leave to dry.

Position the baby chickens on the top of the cake and pipe the inscription in blue-coloured royal icing with a No2 nozzle.

Roll out some sugarpaste thinly. Then cut out the required number of daisies and small blossoms. The centres of the daisies are made with small blossoms. Leave to dry. Paint the flowers with appropriate food colourings. Arrange groups of daisies and blossoms over the cake in a random design, but keeping an overall balance, securing with dots of royal icing.

CARNATIONS

INGREDIENTS

fruit cake baked in 17.5-cm (7-in) oval cake tin (pan)
boiled, sieved apricot jam
600g (1¼lb/2½ cups) marzipan
vodka or other alcohol
600g (1¼lb/2½ cups) sugarpaste
flower modelling paste
50g (2oz/¼ cup) royal icing
carnations
filler blossoms

EQUIPMENT

rolling pin
pastry brush
sharp knife
2 metres (2¼ yards) yellow ribbon, 12-mm (½-in) wide
plastic wrap
large carnation cutter
medium carnation cutter
vegetable parchment piping bags
No0 nozzle
No1 nozzle
No4 nozzle
cocktail stick (toothpick)
scriber
small blossom cutter
paintbrush

This is a quick, simple cake that can be tackled confidently by a beginner with the minimum of equipment. The medium carnation cutter has a dual purpose: it is also used to cut the frilled sections for the top and base of the cake.

Cover the cake with marzipan and sugarpaste in the usual way and place on the board. Measure the circumference of the iced cake with a tape so that you can calculate the number of sections needed to make the frilled base decoration. Attach yellow ribbon around the base of the cake and the edge of the board.

Roll out some flower modelling paste very thinly. Using a large carnation cutter, cut out several petals and cut each one into two pieces. Cover the pieces with plastic wrap to prevent their drying out before they are decorated. Using the tip of a No4 writing nozzle as a cutter, make eyelet holes in each one. Frill the curved edge with a cocktail stick (toothpick), outline the holes and pipe any additional decoration in royal icing with a No0 nozzle. Repeat this procedure with the remaining half petals.

When the pieces are dry, attach the straight edges with dots of icing to the top of the ribbon with the frilled part resting on the board, to form a continuous row around the base of the cake.

Mark a line with a scriber about 2.5cm (1in) from the edge of the top of the cake. Using a medium carnation cutter, cut out more petals and proceed as for the base petals. Position the half petals with the straight edges against the scribed line.

Neaten the edges by piping a row of dots in royal icing with a No1 nozzle on both the top and base half petals.

Decorate the top of the cake with carnations and filler blossoms, cutting off the wires short and sticking them into small balls of sugarpaste set at regular intervals inside the petal border.

To work the embroidery on the side of the cake, use a small blossom cutter to emboss the flower shape in the paste, pressing lightly to make a mark without cutting too deeply. With a No0 nozzle and pale yellow-coloured royal icing, outline one petal and brush with a damp paintbrush from the outside edge towards the centre of the flowers. Make a hole in the centre of each flower with a paintbrush handle and outline in white royal icing with a No0 nozzle.

FRANGIPANI

INGREDIENTS

fruit cake baked in 20-cm (8-in) heart-shaped cake tin (pan)
boiled, sieved apricot jam
700g (1½lb/3 cups) marzipan
vodka or other alcohol
700g (1½lb/3 cups) sugarpaste
royal icing
spray of frangipani
filler blossoms
leaves

EQUIPMENT

25-cm (10-in) heart-shaped cake board
rolling pin
sharp knife
pastry brush
embossing tool
greaseproof paper
adhesive tape
scriber
circular Garrett frill cutter
cocktail stick (toothpick)
ribbon insert cutter or fine pointed knife
1 metre (1 yard) white ribbon, 6-mm (¼-in) wide
vegetable parchment piping bag
No0 nozzle
3-mm (⅛-in) white ribbon loops and trails

Creamy-coloured frangipani is a popular choice for a silver or pearl wedding anniversary.

Cover the cake with marzipan and sugarpaste in the usual way. Cover the board with sugarpaste. Carefully lift the cake on to the board. Decorate the sugarpaste round the edge of the board with an embossing tool.

Cut a strip of greaseproof paper of the same length and depth as the side of the cake. Fold into six sections and cut a curve in one edge to the depth required for the frill. Wrap the strip of paper around the cake and secure with adhesive tape. Mark a guideline for the frill with a scriber.

Pipe a row of beading around the base of the cake. Cut out circles of sugarpaste with a circular Garrett frill cutter and cut holes in the centres. Open out each circle and frill one edge by rolling a cocktail stick (toothpick) back and forth to stretch it. This will give the necessary fullness. Moisten the plain edges of each frill and attach to the cake along the guideline, taking care to make the points neat and sharp. Distribute the fullness evenly.

Using a ribbon insert cutter or a fine pointed knife cut evenly spaced slits for ribbon inserts above the frill. Cut the 6-mm (¼-in) wide ribbon into short lengths and insert the ends of each one into two slits. Using a No0 nozzle pipe some decorative details between the ribbon inserts and across the top of the frill to disguise the join. Pipe fine embroidery around the side of the cake, above the frill.

Make an arrangement of flowers, leaves and ribbon loops and trails on top of the cake.

The run-out numerals on the top of the cake have been painted with silver confectioners' paint. This is used for items which can be removed from the cake when it is cut and should not be eaten.

HONEYSUCKLE AND BRIAR ROSES WEDDING CAKE

INGREDIENTS

*fruit cakes baked in 15-cm (6-in), 20-cm (8-in) and
  25-cm (10-in) square cake tins (pans)*
boiled, sieved apricot jam
2.2kg (4½lb/9 cups) marzipan
vodka or other alcohol
*2.2kg (4½lb/9 cups) sugarpaste, plus 700g (1½lbs/
  3 cups) for the boards*
dark brown food colouring
egg yellow food colouring
green food colouring
paprika food colouring
royal icing
8 large briar roses
6 briar rose buds
6 sprays of honeysuckle
bell flowers
small carnations
daisies
small filler blossoms
ivy leaves

EQUIPMENT

*20-cm (8-in), 25-cm (10-in) and 35-cm (14-in)
  square cake boards*
rolling pin
pastry brush
sharp knife
greaseproof paper
scriber
vegetable parchment piping bags
No0 nozzle
No1 nozzle
*2.5 metres (2¾ yards) cream satin ribbon, 6-mm (¼-in)
  wide*

Cover the cakes with marzipan in the usual way. The shade of the sugarpaste is achieved by using a little egg yellow food colouring and a trace of dark brown. Add the colouring to a small piece of sugarpaste and then knead this thoroughly into the remaining sugarpaste. Before using, cut the sugarpaste in half to ensure that there are no streaks. Food colouring tends to make sugarpaste dry with a greater likelihood of crazing so it should be used immediately after mixing. Cover the cakes with sugarpaste. Place the iced cakes on the boards. If liked, the boards may also be iced.

Cut a strip of greaseproof paper 3.75-cm (1½-in) wide and long enough to reach diagonally from one corner of the bottom tier to another. Lay the strip over the cake from the bottom right-hand corner to the top left-hand corner and mark the edges with a scriber. Then lay the strip of paper on the middle tier from bottom left to top right and mark the edges as before. Make a template of the honeysuckle pattern and transfer the outline to the left of the diagonal strip on the bottom tier and the right on the middle tier.

With a No0 nozzle and cream-coloured royal icing, fill both diagonal strips with cornelli work. Pipe neat edges with a slightly darker-coloured icing. The honeysuckle design is piped with a No0 nozzle and green-, cream- and peach-coloured royal icing in satin stitch (*see page 7*). This stitch is only used where a design requires narrow bands of colour.

Attach cream ribbon around the base of each cake, securing with dots of royal icing. Pipe a bead border with a No1 nozzle around the base of each cake.

Make a template of the top of the top tier of the cake. Draw a line about 2.5-cm (1-in) from each edge, forming a square. Draw another line inside, forming a square border 2.5-cm (1-in) wide. Cut away the centre leaving a 2.5-cm (1-in) wide border. Lay this diagonally on the top of the cake and mark the outlines with a scriber. With a No0 nozzle and cream-coloured royal icing, fill the border with cornelli work and pipe the edge with slightly darker icing.

Make two loose informal arrangements to show off these simple flowers at their best. The ends should trail over the front edges of the cakes and the sprays should be inserted in holders (*see page 48*). The top tier is decorated with a posy consisting of two briar roses with two buds, two sprays of honeysuckle, two single flowers and buds and a few small filler blossoms and leaves.

SARAH'S CAKE

INGREDIENTS

*fruit cakes baked in 15-cm (6-in), 20-cm (8-in) and
    25-cm (10-in) round tins (pans)*
boiled, sieved apricot jam
2.2kg (4½lb/9 cups) marzipan
vodka or other alcohol
*2.2kg (4½lb/9 cups) sugarpaste, plus 700g (1½lb/
    3 cups) for the boards*
extension work royal icing (see page 36)
pink food colouring
open roses
stephanotis
lilies-of-the-valley

EQUIPMENT

*22.5cm (9-in), 27.5-cm (11-in) and 35-cm (14-in)
    round cake boards*
spiral cake stand
rolling pin
pastry brush
sharp knife
vegetable parchment piping bags
No0 nozzle
No1 nozzle
greaseproof paper
scriber
waxed paper or plastic wrap
wooden skewer
plastic drinking straw or holder

Coat the cake boards with sugarpaste and leave to set for several days. Cover the cakes with marzipan and then sugarpaste in the usual way. Lift the iced cakes on to the boards and smooth out any marks. Pipe a fine snailstrail with a No1 nozzle around the base of each cake.

Cut strips of greaseproof paper the length of the circumference of each cake. Fold into sections: eight for the bottom tier, six for the middle and six for the top. Draw the shape of the extension work on one section of each strip of paper while folded. Cut away the paper above the marked line and unfold the strips. The scallops will vary very slightly in size on each cake. Wrap the strips of paper around the cakes and mark the tops of the extension work with a scriber and also mark the width of the scallops for the bridgework around the base.

With a No1 nozzle and extension work royal icing pipe seven rows of bridgework, allowing each row to dry before piping the next row. With a No0 nozzle, pipe the extension work. When dry, add hailspots in pink-coloured royal icing. Then finish the bottom edge of the extension work with small dots or loops. Using a No0 nozzle and pink-coloured royal icing, pipe fine embroidery above the extension work.

Using a No0 nozzle and white royal icing pipe lace pieces on waxed paper or plastic wrap and leave to dry. Attach lace pieces to the top of the extension work with dots of royal icing. Mark the position for the lace pieces on the top of each cake with a scriber and arrange them in position.

The sprays of open roses, stephanotis and lily-of-the-valley may be laid on the cakes in situ or inserted in holders (*see page 48*). Attach a dome of sugarpaste to the centre of the top tier, and use to secure the flowers, cutting the stem wires quite short and keeping the large roses to the lower part of the arrangement.

AZALEA WEDDING CAKE

INGREDIENTS

fruit cakes baked in 15-cm (6-in), 20-cm (8-in) and 25-cm (10-in) round cake tins (pans)
boiled, sieved apricot jam
2.2kg (4½lb/9 cups) marzipan
vodka or other alcohol
2.2kg (4½lb/9 cups) sugarpaste, plus 700g (1½lb/ 3 cups) for the boards
royal icing
modelling paste
azaleas
small filler blossoms
egg white

EQUIPMENT

20-cm (8-in), 27.5-cm (11-in) and 35-cm (14-in) round cake boards
6–8 round hollow pillars or spiral cake stand
rolling pan
pastry brush
sharp knife
2 metres (2¼ yards) white satin ribbon, 6-mm (¼-in) wide
vegetable parchment piping bags
No0 nozzle
No1 nozzle
greaseproof paper
adhesive tape
pins
fine bridal tulle
curved length of cardboard, such as centre of kitchen paper roll cut in half
plastic wrap
cocktail stick (toothpick)
foam sponge
stamens

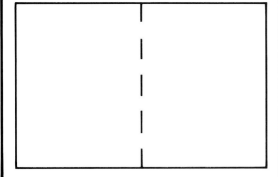

Cover the cakes with marzipan in the usual way. Cover the boards with sugarpaste and leave for a few days to set. Cover the cakes with sugarpaste and place on the boards. Attach 6-mm (¼-in) white satin ribbon around the base of each cake, securing with dots of royal icing. Pipe a snailstrail in royal icing with a No1 nozzle.

Make a template of the lace piece and pin to several thicknesses of tulle. Cut out carefully. Twenty-four shapes are needed for the bottom tier, sixteen for the middle and twelve for the top. Make several more templates of the lace pieces and attach to the outside of a curved length of cardboard with a little royal icing. Cover the templates with separate pieces of plastic wrap.

Half-fill a parchment piping bag with royal icing. The icing should be firm enough not to lose its shape, but soft enough to stick to the tulle. Using a No0 nozzle, hold a tulle shape over a template while piping enough of the floral design to secure it. Complete the design and outline. Repeat until all the tulle shapes have been iced. Leave to dry.

Cut strips of greaseproof paper the length of the circumference of each cake. Fold the strip for the top tier twelve times, the one for the middle tier sixteen times and the one for the bottom twenty-four times, pressing the creases sharply. Unfold each strip and wrap round the relevant cakes. Using a scriber, mark the positions for the tulle pieces. Gently peel away the plastic wrap from the curved tulle pieces. Pipe a little icing at the base of each shape, a dot at the point and press lightly to secure to the sides of the cakes. Decorate the sides of the cakes with dainty embroidery.

To make the prayer book for the top of the cake, roll out some modelling paste about 3-mm (⅛-in) thick. Make a template of the design and cut out in the paste. Make a crease down the centre and dry over two curved shapes to form the cover. Roll out some more paste very thinly and cut out a rectangle the size of the inner part of the template. Curl a corner around a cocktail stick (toothpick). Before the paste is completely dry, remove the cocktail stick and attach the curled page to the cover by brushing a little egg white down the central crease only. When completely dry, pipe an appropriate inscription.

Make a small plaque from modelling paste and position on the top of the cake. Attach the prayer book with a little icing and surround with azaleas and small filler blossoms.

Using a template of the butterfly, cut out tulle shapes, remembering to reverse half of them for the opposite wings. Place plastic wrap over the template and cover with the tulle shapes. Use pins to hold in position while piping. Pipe the decoration and outlines and leave to dry. Pipe the bodies with firm icing and attach the dried wings, supporting with foam sponge until dry. Stick small pieces of stamen to represent the antennae. Attach the butterflies to the cake with dots of royal icing.

Arrange sprays of azaleas, filler blossoms and ribbon loops attractively on the bottom and middle tiers.

A COUNTRY WEDDING

INGREDIENTS

fruit cakes baked in 17.5-cm (7-in), 22.5-cm (9-in)
and 27.5-cm (11-in) round cake tins (pans)
boiled, sieved apricot jam
2.4kg (5¼lb/10½ cups) marzipan
vodka or other alcohol
2.4kg (5¼lb/10½ cups) royal icing
roses
scabious
cornflowers
gypsophila

EQUIPMENT

25-cm (10-in), 30-cm (12-in) and 35-cm (14-in)
round cake boards
spiral cake stand
rolling pin
pastry brush
sharp knife
greaseproof paper
adhesive tape
scriber
tilting turntable
vegetable parchment piping bags
No1 nozzle
No2 nozzle
No3 nozzle
No42 rope nozzle
No43 rope nozzle
No44 rope nozzle
waxed paper
flower nail

Cover the cakes with marzipan using the method for royal icing. Centre each cake on the appropriate board, securing each with a little apricot jam. Coat each cake with white royal icing; for soft cutting, 5ml (1 tsp) glycerine can be added to each 450g (1lb/1½ cups) icing. Leave to dry thoroughly. Using a sharp knife, scrape off any uneven patches of icing and give each cake two more coats to achieve a perfect finish. Coat the exposed edges of each board with royal icing. Leave to dry.

Cut a strip of greaseproof paper of the same length as the circumference of each cake and 12-mm (½-in) less in depth. Make templates of the patterns for the side decorations and use as a guideline to mark the scallops on the strips of paper. Wrap the strips around the relevant cakes, securing them with adhesive tape. Mark the guidelines with a scriber.

Either use a tilting turntable or wedge the cakes at an angle. Using a No3 nozzle, pipe over the guidelines on each cake, with the cake tilted away from you. Leave to dry. Using a No2 nozzle, pipe a line exactly on top of the first lines and another line alongside and quite close to the first lines. Using a No1 nozzle, pipe a line exactly on top of the first two, then another line alongside. You should have three lines, one on top of the other, then two lines and finally a single one.

With a rope nozzle, pipe a neat shell edge around the tops and bases of each cake. Use a No44 nozzle for the bottom tier, a No43 for the middle and a No42 for the top. With a No1 nozzle, overpipe, forming small loops around the shells.

To make the birds, pipe sets of wings on waxed paper and leave to dry. Pipe the bodies in position on the cake and fix a wing in place while the body is wet.

When piping roses, the icing must be very stiff so that the flower can hold its shape. Cut a small square of waxed paper and stick to a flower nail with a dot of royal icing. Hold the nail in your left hand and the piping bag with a medium petal nozzle in a vertical position with the wide end touching the waxed paper, in your right hand.

Turn the nail in an anti-clockwise direction, at the same time squeezing out a ribbon of pink-coloured royal icing to form a complete circle, to make a small cone for the centre of the rose. For the second petal, hold the nozzle at the same angle of 90° to the nail, wide end at the bottom. Squeeze out a petal with the nozzle touching the nail, lifting, then lowering again before pulling the nozzle away. Pipe two more petals, thus forming a bud. For a full-blown rose, pipe another row of five petals, but tilt the nozzle slightly outwards to give the flower a more open look.

Take the rose off the nail, and leave to dry on the waxed paper while piping more flowers. Left-handed people will need to use a special left-handed nozzle and reverse the instructions.

Attach some roses to the centre of each scalloped panel on the sides of each cake, securing with dots of royal icing. Finish the side decoration with piped leaves and small embroidered flowers.

To make the leaves, put a little royal icing in a piping bag without a nozzle and cut the end into a sharp V-shape. As the icing is squeezed directly on to the cake, the point of the bag will form the main vein in the centre of each leaf. Squeeze out a bulb of icing, moving the bag out in the direction of the point, then relax the pressure, which forms the point.

The arrangement of moulded flowers on the top tier consists of roses, scabious, cornflowers and gypsophila to complement the flowers carried by the bride.

See overleaf for patterns

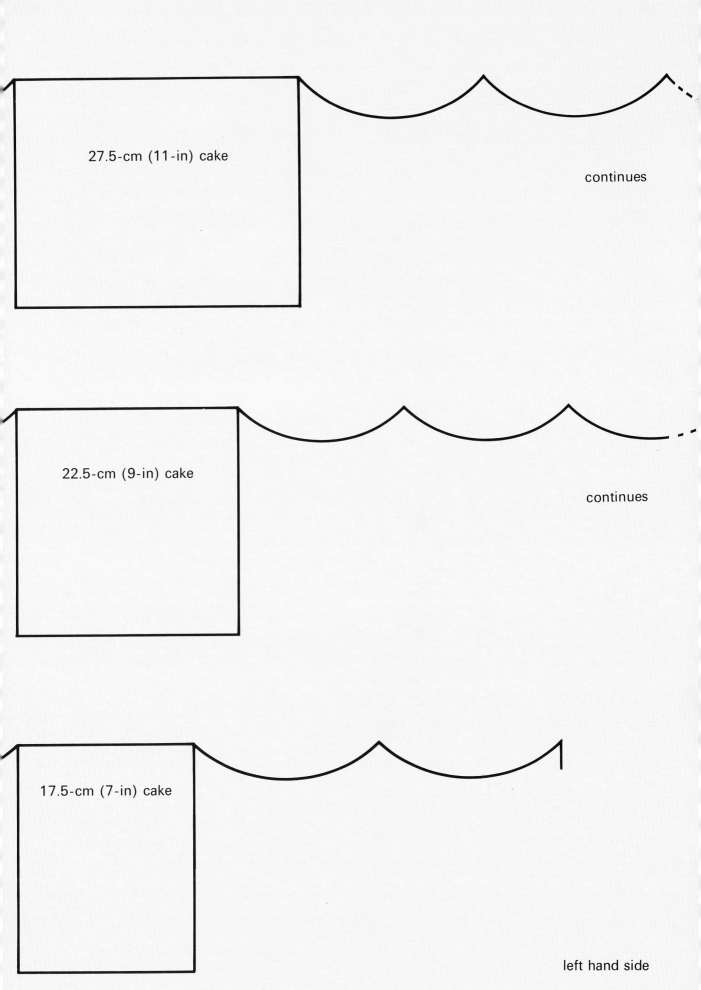

27.5-cm (11-in) cake

continues

22.5-cm (9-in) cake

continues

17.5-cm (7-in) cake

left hand side

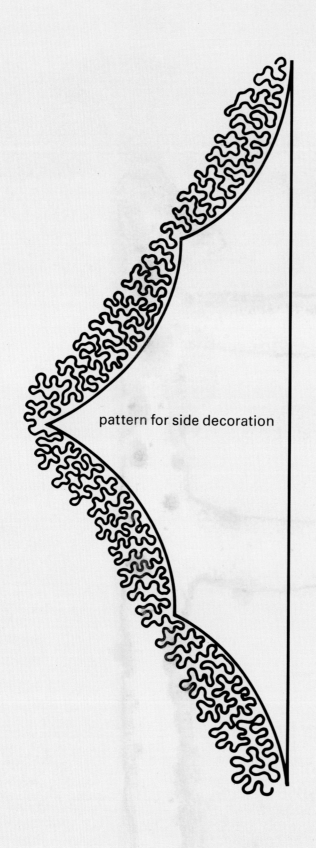

pattern for side decoration

FLORAL FILIGREE *(see page 26)*